A PRACTICAL GUIDE TO

SELECTING A
SMALL
DOG

**An Illustrated guide designed to help you choose
the most suitable small dog for you and your
home from over 80 international breeds**

JOAN PALMER

Long-haired Dachshunds

Press

019

A Salamander Book

©1987 Salamander Books Ltd.,
52 Bedford Row,
London WC1R 4LR
United Kingdom.

ISBN 3-923880-79-0

Library of Congress No. 87-050363

Publishers note: Some material in this
book has previously appeared in *A Dog
of Your Own* and *An Illustrated Guide to
Dogs*.

Credits

Editors: Geoff Rogers, Charlotte
Mortensson
Designers: Roger Hyde, Paul Johnson
Colour artwork: John Francis (Linden
Artists), John Green (John Martin &
Artists) © Salamander Books Ltd.
Line drawings: Glenn Steward (John
Martin & Artists) © Salamander
Books Ltd.
Filmset: Modern Text Typesetting Ltd.,
England
Colour reproductions: Bantam Litho
Ltd., England

Printed in Portugal

Picture Credits

The publishers wish to thank the following photographers and agencies who have
supplied photographs for this book.

Animal Photography Ltd.
6, 12, 13, 21, 22, 23, 26, 38, 40, 46, 48,
77, 78, 81, 83, 84, 85, 86, 88, 92, 95, 99,
100, 101, 103, 104, 105, 106, 107, 108,
113, 114

Marc Henrie
Front cover, back cover, 3, 10, 11, 15,
19, 20, 30, 34, 35, 44, 45, 50, 51, 52, 94,
111, 116

C.P. Keizer (Griffonclub)
117

Robert Pearcy
96

Anne Roslin-Williams
110

Syndication International
7, 8, 9, 25, 39, 47, 76, 93, 112

Contents

Text and colour illustrations are cross-referenced throughout as follows: 52▶
The breeds are arranged in order of increasing weight. Page numbers in Roman type refer to text entries; those in **bold** to colour illustrations.

Introduction

There are many advantages to owning a small dog. It eats less than its larger contemporaries and is therefore not such a drain on the household budget. Also it does not take up much space and is better suited than say, an Afghan Hound or Old English Sheepdog to a smaller house and garden. Some toy breeds can even adapt happily to apartment life because their exercise requirements are so modest.

It would, however, be wrong to assume that because a dog is diminutive it does not enjoy a good walk. A study of the breed profiles in this book will show that while some fairly small dogs, such as the amiable but rather fierce-looking French Bulldog, will adopt a take-it or leave-it attitude towards exercise, the imperial Pekingese will readily walk for very long distances.

Small dogs, such as the Tibetan Spaniel or the Cavalier King Charles Spaniel, the biggest of the toys, are ideal companions for children and are not as likely to cause them to fall over in play as a bigger dog might do. On the other hand, toy breeds can often prove to be snappy if provoked and are susceptible to injury if dropped by tiny, inexperienced hands. However, toy dogs do make wonderful companions for the elderly and are appreciative lap dogs.

When choosing a pet which is also to perform guarding duties, a small dog can be just as effective as a more traditional guarding breed—few people can distinguish between the furious barking of a Dachshund and that of a traditional guarding breed such as a Dobermann from behind a closed front door.

Many small breeds are blessed with supreme intelligence and some, like the Shetland Sheepdog, give a good account of themselves in obedience work. Others do well in the show ring, to which they can be easily transported because of their small size. Yet another advantage of owning a small dog is that many live to an old age—fifteen or even sixteen years is not unusual.

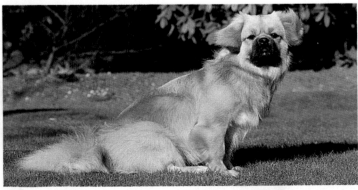

Above: The Tibetan Spaniel is a playful companion for children.

Above: These Shetland Sheepdog puppies are now ready to go to their new home.

When choosing a small dog, it is vital to realize that as well as coming in different shapes and sizes, small dogs have individual characteristics and needs. Terriers, for example, are vivacious dogs which were bred to hunt small mammals and, although they can be lots of fun to own, they are not the ideal choice for the elderly or sedate, who might be happier with a gentle, companionable gundog, or a dog which has been bred for no other purpose than to be an affectionate companion and pet.

It is also essential to bear in mind your own lifestyle and environment when selecting a dog. For instance, someone who is especially houseproud will not want a dog with a long coat that sheds hairs on the carpet. Expense should also be taken into account when selecting breeds which require regular trips to the grooming parlour.

Buying Your Small Dog
Once you have decided on the breed you want to own you should write to your national kennel club asking for the names and addresses of breeders of that variety. You may also like to query dates and venues of dog shows to be held in your area. Attending one or two shows should enable you to examine at close range the breed—or breeds—which have taken your fancy, to ask the breeders any questions you may have, and to enquire if they will soon have a litter available.

If you have set you heart on an unusual variety, don't expect to find a breeder living a short drive away. Although there are more breeders of small dogs living in towns than there are of big dogs, it may be necessary to travel some distance to obtain your pet.

Dog or Bitch?
An important decision you will need to make is whether to buy a dog or a bitch. Both sexes make good pets. The bitch usually has a gentler nature than the dog, she is almost always chosen for obedience work and makes a reliable child's companion. The

dog has a more rumbustious nature and is constantly attracted to the opposite sex, unlike the bitch which does not look for a suitor except during her twice-yearly season. It is a matter of personal choice.

Pet or Show Dog?

People often make the mistake of thinking that because their dog has a certificate of pedigree it can be termed a show dog and could be expected to win prizes in the show ring. This is not the case. A certificate of pedigree proves only that a dog is the progeny of a sire and dam of the same breed with a line that can be traced back for some generations.

Each pure bred canine variety has what is known as a Breed Standard laid down by its national kennel club. The Standard clearly sets out those characteristics and physical attributes which add up to a perfect specimen of the breed, for instance, the desired temperament, coat colour and texture, height, weight and other points. The exhibit which conforms most exactly with its Standard will be picked out by an experienced judge in the show ring.

The majority of pure bred dogs are not show dogs. This is no reflection on their beauty of form or their temperament. The fact that they are a fraction too large or too small, have a tail which is set too high or too low, or a mouth which is slightly undershot or overshot, may have barred them from competing against their fellows.

If you think that you would like a dog which you can enter in dog shows you should ask the breeder to pick out a likely prospect for you, but remember that not only is the price of a future show dog likely to be reflected in the asking price, but there can be no guarantees as to the animal's future success.

Above: The lively Pomeranian needs daily grooming and should only be purchased by those who are prepared to spend lots of time on their pet.

Above: The tiny Griffon Bruxellois adapts well to town life as it does not need a great deal of exercise.

A reputable breeder will, based on their knowledge of the breed, do their best to select a promising show puppy for you. However, a puppy is usually purchased at eight to ten weeks of age and it is generally six months or more before the way in which it will develop can be forecast with any degree of certainty.

Documents
When you buy your puppy the breeder should give you the certificate of pedigree and a signed transfer form enabling you to record the change of ownership with the national kennel club. This is most important. If your dog is not correctly registered you are likely to run into difficulty should you wish to enter it in shows, breed from your bitch or, if you have selected a male dog, advertise it for stud purposes.

You should ask the breeder about the puppy's worming programme and whether it has had its vaccinations. If these have been administered you will need the record card which will advise you when the recommended booster inoculations are due. If you are intending to exhibit the puppy when it reaches six months of age and is eligible to be entered in show classes, you may decide to ask the breeder for information about the specialist breed club. This latter information will also be available from your national kennel club.

A reliable breeder will have no objection to the purchase being made subject to a veterinary examination. If the dog is discovered to be unfit, it should be—and is by law in the United Kingdom—returnable to the source of purchase for a full refund of the money paid. However, a veterinary certificate stating the reason for return must be produced. Adult dogs should be bought with a seven or fourteen day warranty.

Most breeders are only too happy to volunteer a service such as this and those who do not do so should be regarded with suspicion. Genuine dog breeders value their good reputation and the name of their kennels.

Feeding Small Dogs

Before you take your puppy home you should make sure that it is properly weaned, that is, able to take both milk and solid food.

Breeders usually encourage a litter to start taking solid food from about three weeks of age. However, it is unlikely that the pups will be completely weaned until they are six or seven weeks old. (It is inadvisable to purchase a puppy under eight weeks of age, and you should not allow yourself to be persuaded to do so.)

The breeder should give you a diet sheet for the puppy which you should strictly adhere to for the first fortnight, gradually introducing any changes thereafter. Breakfast and supper may consist of a dry, branded baby food mixed with milk and a little sugar and the evening feed could be an egg whisked in milk. However, lunch and tea should comprise of a meat meal, for example a saucerful of lightly cooked lean, minced beef supplemented by puppy meal or biscuit in the proportion of three parts meat to two parts biscuit.

As a rule of thumb, puppies should receive four meals a day until they are three months of age—breakfast, lunch, tea and supper, because at this stage they cannot digest their total food requirement in one ration. When the puppy reaches four months old the evening meal can be omitted and at six months breakfast can be stopped. By the time your puppy is one year old it should only have one meal a day, but because many small breeds have

Above: Lakeland Terrier pups will grow into loveable, but very energetic dogs.

Above: The long-coated Chihuahua has, in recent years, become more popular than the smooth-coated variety.

such tiny stomachs, their owners often prefer to give them their rations in the form of two daily feeds, even in adult life.

It is important to point out that some small breeds require a larger or smaller food intake than others in the early months of life. If you are in any doubt as to your puppy's development you should consult your veterinarian.

You will note from the breed profiles the expected weight of an adult dog. However, many breeds, notably Chihuahuas and Yorkshire Terriers, grow to be larger and heavier than their breed standards and therefore require more food.

Don't fall into the trap of giving your pet scraps from the table at your own meal-times. It is a practice that can only result in a dog with a ruined waistline as well as becoming a pest, pawing for attention whenever there is food to hand. However, do make sure that your dog's food is offered at the same time each day. Dogs are creatures of habit and look forward to their meal as much as we look forward to our own.

Although the feeding of scraps is not recommended, there is no objection to offering tit-bits on a reward basis in training, particularly in the early stages.

Branded Pet Foods
In the past, dog owners were often suspicious of prepared pet food products. Nowadays, branded pet foods are scientifically produced to meet all the nutritional requirements of the dog and this method of feeding has been adopted by a vast number of dog owners. However, it is essential to read the instructions to ascertain whether the product is a complete food or is one to which another product such as biscuit meal, must be added.

It is quite acceptable to wean puppies directly on to a diet of specially branded puppy food and many owners prefer to do this.

Above: Puppy owners will find an indoor pen invaluable for house training and for confining their pets for short periods of time.

Exercise and Good Health
Before taking your dog for a walk outside, it is essential that it should have been vaccinated against the main killer diseases—distemper, infectious hepatitis, two forms of leptospirosis and canine parvovirus. It will also need booster inoculations at regular intervals thereafter.

Highly effective vaccines, free from side effects, are now available to combat these diseases and are usually administered at about nine to ten weeks of age, consisting of two injections with a two to three week interval in between. There is also a vaccine against rabies which is recommended for dogs living in countries where this scourge is endemic. In some countries, such as the United States, rabies vaccinations are required by law. They are unnecessary in rabies-free zones such as Australasia and the United Kingdom.

Regular worming is also necessary. Puppies should be wormed at intervals of one to two weeks from three weeks of age until they are six months old. Thereafter, they should be wormed every six months. However, the recommended treatment can vary in different parts of the world and it is as well to seek the guidance of a veterinarian.

Once your puppy has had its vaccinations you can enjoy taking it out for exercise although you should not attempt really long or strenuous walks until the pup is six months old.

Although most small breeds will happily exercise themselves in the garden or yard, and enjoy retrieving balls and other playthings, they do, almost without exception, look forward to a daily walk. Once a routine has been established, they will remind you by going to fetch their lead or sitting by the door at the appointed hour.

Of course, one of the great advantages of owning a small breed is that it is so easily carried in a pet dog carrier, or even a shopping basket, if a walk proves to be that little bit too far.

Sometimes people imagine, quite wrongly, that it is unkind to confine a small dog in any type of box or carrying case. In fact, almost every breeder of the smaller varieties has specially constructed boxes for them to sleep and be transported in, the dogs enjoying the comfort and, above all, security of being safely shut away for short periods out of the reach of large people and frightening noises. Also, while there are many places where it is forbidden to take a small dog on a lead, objections are seldom raised to a small dog in a carrying case or basket.

Another useful item of equipment which the intending dog owner may wish to buy is an indoor pen made of plastic or wire mesh. Such pens are easily constructed and are ideal for house training and for when the owner has to go out for a short while. The pen is lined with paper and the puppy's bed, toys and water-bowl are placed inside. A puppy will rarely, if ever, soil its own bed and the paper can be easily disposed of when the occupant is released after its short stay. The pen will also be of use if you decide to take your pet to shows as it will fold flat in the boot of your car.

It cannot be over-emphasized that small breeds are rarely kennelled out of doors—indeed toy varieties should never be. Small dogs require the comfort of a basket in a draught free position indoors.

The small dog will perform many roles whether as show dog, obedience dog, sportsman or guard. Above all, however, it is a loyal companion which will want to share its owner's life.

Above: Dog-carrying boxes are the best way of transporting small dogs.

CHIHUAHUA (Long-coat and Smooth-coat)

Good points
- *Ideal for town dwellers*
- *Intensely loyal and affectionate*
- *Keenly intelligent*
- *Guard dog in miniature*
- *Inexpensive to keep*

Take heed
- *May snap at teasing children*
- *Strong willed*
- *Hates the cold*

The Chihuahua is keenly intelligent, fiercely protective and cheap to keep. Also, being the world's tiniest dog, it is the least likely to fall foul of the landlord.

The adult Chihuahua usually takes a few weeks to reveal its true personality, keeping its new owner under careful surveillance, perhaps giving the impression that it is shy. Actually, it is weighing up which of them is to be master in the home!

Size
Weight between 0.9-2.7kg/2-6lb (under 1.8kg/4lb preferred for show). There is no desired height in this breed's standard.

Exercise
Contrary to belief, the Chihuahua is ready, and able, to walk as far as most owners would wish, although it doesn't object to an occasional ride in a shopping basket. The fact that its exercise requirements are moderate makes this breed an ideal choice of pet for the elderly.

Grooming
The Chihuahua should be groomed with a soft brush. A rub down with the proverbial velvet glove, or pad, will make the coat gleam. Nails must be regularly clipped and the ears kept clean.

Feeding
The requirement of a very small Chihuahua should be 57-85g (2-3oz) of cooked minced beef or branded dog food, with a handful of puppy biscuits. These dogs fare best on two or three small meals rather than one large daily feed. Bigger specimens can manage up to ½ can (376g, 13.3oz size) of branded dog food, or the equivalent, and a handful of dog biscuits.

Health care
Not as delicate as one might imagine, but they dislike the cold and appreciate a coat to keep them warm when out of doors in winter. These dogs are definitely not designed for kennel living.

Watch out for the molera, a small opening on top of the skull. The Chihuahua's molera, unlike that of a human baby, may never fill in, so a blow on the head could prove fatal. This breed is prone to 'snorts'; a spasm can often be cured by lifting the pet purposefully up and down. They also have a tendency to shiver, a habit that evokes sympathy from onlookers and generally makes the owner seem the villain of the piece, folk wrongly imagining that the Chihuahua is terrifed or frozen.

Origin and history
Named after the state of Chihuahua in Mexico, the Chihuahua is believed to have been the sacred dog of the Incas. Nevertheless, it seems likely that a few may have been used by the American Indians in their cooking pots. There is also a theory that Chihuahuas were once fierce little dogs living in holes in the ground, which could well account for their inclination to huddle together in every warm nook and cranny.

55▶

PAPILLON (And Phalène)

Good points
- *Affectionate*
- *Dainty size*
- *Good house dog*
- *Trainable for competitive obedience*
- *Usually strong and healthy*

Take heed
- *Not keen on visitors*
- *Possessive towards owners*

The Papillon is a toy spaniel that takes its name from the French word for 'butterfly'. The breed is often referred to as the 'Butterfly Dog' because of the manner in which its ears are set on the head, fringed like a butterfly's wings. The Phalène is identical except that the ears are dropped, and this variety is known as the 'moth'.

The Papillon is an affectionate, lively little dog. It is resilient, whelps easily, is a good walker, and can adapt to extremes of climate. Its attractive appearance and friendly nature make it the ideal family pet. But, like many toy breeds, it has a tendency to be possessive towards its owners and often resents visitors to the home.

Size
The ideal height at the withers is 20-28cm (8-11in). The dog will appear to be slightly longer than high when properly furnished with ruff and hind fringes.

Exercise
Like quite a number of toy breeds, the Papillon will happily walk its owner off his feet, or be content with a walk around the park. One thing is sure: you won't tire it!

Grooming
Daily grooming is required to keep this breed in good condition.

Feeding
Recommended would be ⅓-½ can (376g, 13.3oz size) of a branded meaty product, with biscuit added in equal part by volume; or 1-1½ cups of a dry food, complete diet,

Above: The dainty and affectionate Papillon — ideal for limited space.

mixed in the proportion of 1 cup to ½ cup of hot or cold water.

Origin and history
Believed to be a descendant of the Dwarf Spaniel of the 16th century and to have originated in Spain, the dainty little Papillon has been included in many paintings, including some by Rubens and Van Dyke. The Phalène, or Continental Toy Spaniel, is identical except for its drop ears. In the United States and the United Kingdom they are judged as one breed with almost identical standards except for colour variations, but specimens over 30cm (12in) cannot be shown in America.

The French Fédération Cynologique Internationale (FCI) separates the breeds by both type and weight variations, those over 2.5kg (5½lb) in weight entering a separate class. Papillons have done well in obedience classes. 55▶

POMERANIAN

Good points
- *Adaptable*
- *Devoted to owner*
- *Handy size*
- *Happy nature*
- *Ideal for apartment living*

Take heed
- *Will yap if unchecked*
- *Thinks it is a 'big' dog, so bigger dogs may be provoked!*

The Pomeranian is a happy, active little dog that will adapt cheerfully to life in a one-roomed apartment or a spacious dwelling, revelling in the role of lap dog or enjoying walks with its owner. Alternatively, it will amuse itself adequately in a garden. It makes a faithful and devoted companion.

Size
Dog 1.8-2kg (4-4½lb); bitch 2-2.5kg (4½-5½lb).

Exercise
It is wrong to think that toy breeds are of use for little else except sitting decoratively on their owner's knees, and the Pomeranian is no exception. True, they adore being pampered and petted, but they are also lively little dogs, quite able to walk as far as their owner would wish — often further. Alternatively, they will exercise themselves quite happily in a garden.

Grooming
This is not the breed for those who cannot spare the time for daily grooming. Indeed, the Pomeranian has two coats to care for: a short fluffy under-coat, and a long straight top-coat covering the whole of the body. Daily brushing with a stiff brush is a must. The coat should be damped with cold water, and the moisture rubbed in with the fingertips; finally the dog is rubbed down with a towel.

Working from the head, part the coat and brush it forward from roots to tips. Make a further parting and repeat this procedure until the whole dog has been covered.

The Pomeranian requires regular trimming; obtain advice from a breeder or breed club as to how this should be carried out.

Feeding
Recommended would be ⅓-½ can (376g, 13.3oz size) of a branded meaty product, with biscuit added in equal part by volume; or 1-1½ cups of dry food, complete diet, mixed in the proportion of 1 cup to ½ cup of hot or cold water.

Origin and history
The Pomeranian takes its name from Pomerania, in Germany, and is generally thought to be of mid-European origin. However, it is a member of the Spitz family, which could mean that its history began in the Arctic Circle.

The known history of the breed dates from the mid-18th century when it was introduced to several European countries. It became very popular until, following the raiding of the Summer Palace in Peking in 1860 and the appearance of the Imperial Pekingese, some of its popularity was usurped by that breed.

The Pomeranian, in those early days, was a very much larger dog, up to 13.6kg (30lb) in weight, and it was bred down until, by 1896, show classes for Pomeranians were divided into those for exhibits over and under 3.6k (8lb). The British Kennel Club withdrew challenge certificates for the over 3.6kg (8lb) variety in 1915. The American Pomeranian club was formed in New York in 1900.55▶

JAPANESE CHIN (Japanese Spaniel)

Good points
- *Affectionate*
- *Loyal family dog*
- *Hardy*
- *Good with children*

Take heed
- *That silky coat tends to shed!*
- *Guard against exertion and overheating in warm weather due to breathing difficulties*

The Japanese Chin (sometimes called Japanese Spaniel), might, at first glance, be mistaken for the Pekingese, and it is possible that the two breeds may have evolved from a common stock. It is, however, a high-stepping, graceful dog that is taller in the leg and has a much lighter body than the Pekingese.

The Japanese Chin, it must be remembered, *is* a 'spaniel' and there are some similarities with the King Charles Spaniel, whose origin can also be traced to Japan. However, it has much more of the perky confidence of the tinier breeds than the slower-moving spaniel, and is a lively but dignified little oriental that likes nothing better than to be the centre of attention and is miserable if its advances are thwarted.

Size
1.8-3.2kg (4-7lb).

Exercise
This is a happy little dog that will delight in going for walks and playing games with all the family. It will walk as far as its owners wish, or be happy with a run in the park. The Japanese Chin is quite tough, despite its delicate structure, and will enjoy careful handling by youngsters. But it does like to climb, so be careful it does not fall.

Grooming
Daily grooming with a pure bristle brush will maintain the Chin's luxurious silky coat in good condition. Always give this breed a bath before a show!

Feeding
170-227g (6-8oz) of cooked minced beef, or ½ can (376g, 13.3oz size) of branded dog food, with a handful of dog biscuits, will keep the Chin in excellent health. Lean meat scraps and the occasional non-splintery bone will be enjoyed and, like most small breeds, the Japanese Chin will find lots of pleasure in doggie chews. Remember that dogs should not be given cakes or sweets.

Origin and history
This breed was, for over 1000 years, a favourite of the Japanese emperors, one of whom decreed that all Japanese Chin should be worshipped; some tiny specimens were even kept in hanging cages in the manner of small oriental birds.

The breed is reputed to have found its way to Europe with returning seamen in medieval times. However, the Japanese Chin did not make its appearance in the British show ring until 1862, and is not recorded as being shown in the United States until 20 years later.

Two Japanese Chin were presented to Queen Victoria by Commodore Perry on his return from the Far East in 1853, and this did much to promote the breed. Although they never gained the popularity of the Pekingese, they had a fairly staunch following up until the First World War, when their numbers diminished. Registrations have been on the increase in recent years, and it has become a dependable show dog. 55▶

SMALL GERMAN SPITZ (Kleinspitz)

Good points
- *Adaptable to town or country*
- *Beautiful*
- *Excellent guard*
- *Loyal companion*
- *Intelligent*
- *Ideal for apartments*

Take heed
- *Likes to bark*
- *Suspicious of strangers*

The Small German Spitz is the small variety of the Great German Spitz (Gross-spitz). The only difference between the types is in size; characteristics and conformation are the same.

This is a happy, extremely intelligent little dog. It makes an excellent companion, does not need a great deal of exercise, and adapts well to life in town or country. It usually loves its owners deeply, but does not care much for strangers. Perhaps its only drawback is that it rather likes the sound of its own voice! It is unlikely to chase sheep: guard duty and the protection of its beloved home are far more important.

Size
Height: 28cm (11in) maximum at withers, weight not more than 3.4kg (7½lb). (The Gross-spitz stands about 40cm [15¾in] high).

Exercise
Despite its ability to cover immense areas at speed, the Spitz does not require a great deal of exercise; members of this variety can live quite happily in a small town house.

Grooming
Vigorous daily brushing is necessary if you don't wish to be always vacuuming your carpet!

Feeding
Recommended would be ⅓-½ can (376g, 13.3oz size) of a branded meaty product, with biscuit added in equal part by volume; or 1-1½ cups of a dry food, complete diet, mixed in the proportion of 1 cup of feed to ½ cup of hot or cold water.

Origin and history
It is difficult to pinpoint the origin of this variety of Spitz, for the prehistoric remains of such types have been found throughout Asia and the Pacific, and drawings of similar dogs were found among the remains of the ancient Pharaohs. There are a number of Spitz varieties, all of which are very similar in character and type. Indeed, in the late Sir Richard Glyn's 'Champion Dogs of the World' (Harrap), reference is made to a white variety of Spitz established in German Pomerania some 160 years ago and bred in different sizes. Some of the smallest size, and of various colours, were introduced into the UK under the name of Pomeranian and became well established.

The larger varieties attracted little attention in Germany or elsewhere until the end of the last century, when a breed club was formed in Germany. The club divided the breed into varieties by colour and size.

About the same time the Russians began to develop the Spitz varieties which were distributed throughout Russia under the name of Laika. A Laika was the first dog sent into Earth orbit.

The Russians divided their standard Laikas into the four subvarieties, the East Siberian, West Siberian, Russian and Russian-Finnish, the latter being the smallest. They are still used as gundogs and hunt elk and bear.

YORKSHIRE TERRIER

Good points
- *Affectionate*
- *Healthy and fearless*
- *Good watchdog*
- *Suits apartment living*

Take heed
- *Lengthy show preparation*
- *Needs weekly bath*
- *Difficult to determine pup's eventual size and colouring*

The Yorkshire Terrier is one of the most popular dogs of the day. It rivals the Chihuahua for the title of the world's smallest dog. It is unlikely to be over-awed by larger animals, however, and is not the ideal choice for the stand-offish, because it wants to make friends with everybody. It has been described as a big dog inhabiting a small dog's body; in fact it thinks it is enormous!

Size
Weight up to 3.2kg (7lb).

Exercise
The Yorkie is well suited to town and apartment living, but will prove tireless on a country walk.

Grooming
Many Yorkie owners are content for their pet to have a somewhat scruffy 'shaggy dog' look as long as they know that it is clean and healthy. The show aspirant, however, has a busy time ahead, for the Yorkshire Terrier is exhibited on a show box, which displays its immaculate coat to advantage, a condition that can be achieved only through endless grooming, shampooing and oiling. The show Yorkie spends much of its life, away from the ring, in curlers!

Feeding
Similar to that of other toy breeds, with four meals given in puppy-hood, reducing to one meal at a year old, comprising ½ can of branded dog food, or the bought meat equivalent (approximately 199-227g, 7-8oz), lightly

Above: The Yorkshire Terrier looks its best when groomed for a show.

cooked and supplemented by biscuits. Lean meat scraps can be given, and bones are appreciated, but never chicken bones.

Health care
The Yorkie has strong, terrier-type teeth, but it is as well to have them scaled by a veterinarian at regular intervals. Toy breeds tend to lose their teeth at an early age (some-times as early as three), but the avoidance of titbits will preserve them for as long as is possible.

Origin and history
The Yorkie is similar in appearance to the Australian (or Sydney) Silky Terrier. It has been with us for little more than 100 years. It is believed that the breed evolved through the crossing of the Skye Terrier with the old Black and Tan Terrier, although it is rumoured that the Maltese Terrier and the Dandie Dinmont Terrier may also have contributed to pro-ducing this game little breed, which is renowned as a brave and efficient ratter. 55▶

MALTESE TERRIER (Maltese)

Good points
- *Adaptable about exercise*
- *Extremely good with children*
- *Healthy*
- *Long-lived*
- *Sensitive*
- *Sweet-natured*

Take heed
- *Needs fastidious daily grooming*

The Maltese Terrier is a good-tempered dog that makes the ideal family pet. It is reliable with children, adaptable about exercise, and usually healthy, and it generally remains playful throughout its long life.

Size
Not over 25cm (10in) from ground to top of shoulder.

Exercise
Can manage a long walk or be content with a stroll in the park.

Grooming
Most important. Use a bristle brush every day from puppyhood and use baby powder on legs and underside to keep the animal clean between baths. Obtain advice from the breeder about show preparation; this breed may not be the ideal choice for new show aspirants.

Feeding
Recommended would be ⅓ can (376g, 13.3oz size) of a branded meaty product, with biscuit added in equal part by volume; or 1-1½ cups of a dry food, complete diet, mixed in the proportion of 1 cup of feed to ½ cup of hot or cold water. Such a diet is, of course, offered purely as a guide. The owner may occasionally substitute lightly cooked minced beef, mixed with biscuit. Water must be available to all breeds at all times.

Origin and history
The Maltese Terrier is described as

Above: Maltese puppies will make reliable companions for children.

the oldest of European toy breeds. However, there is some controversy as to whether it originated in Malta, although the breed has certainly existed there for centuries. The Maltese Terrier also found its way to China and the Philippines, probably due to enterprising Maltese traders.

Like the Papillon, the Maltese has been depicted by many famous artists, including Goya, Rubens, and the famous animal painter Sir Edwin Landseer, who in 1930 produced a portrait entitled *The Lion Dog from Malta — the last of his race,* which shows their rarity on the island at that time. The breed first became established in the United Kingdom during the reign of Henry VIII and was a popular pet among elegant ladies. It had a class of its own for the first time in Birmingham, England, in 1864, since when it has gained popularity in both the United Kingdom and the United States.56 ▶

ITALIAN GREYHOUND

Good points
- *Affectionate*
- *Easy to train*
- *Graceful appearance*
- *Intelligent and obedient*
- *Odourless*
- *Rarely moults*

Take heed
- *Wounded by harsh words*
- *Should not be kept in a kennel*

The Italian Greyhound is the perfect Greyhound in miniature, a graceful dainty animal that makes an ideal house pet. It does, however, need plenty of exercise and will enjoy a day's rabbiting, should the opportunity arise.

Size
The most desirable weight is 2.7-3.6kg (6-8lb), and not exceeding 4.5kg (10lb).

Exercise
Certainly not the dog to keep shut up indoors all day. It thrives on plenty of exercise, but adapts well to town living with adequate walks and off-the-lead runs.

Grooming
The Greyhound needs little more than a rub down with a silk handkerchief. But remember that this breed feels the cold, hates the wind and rain, and needs a coat. Care must be taken of the teeth.

Below: The Italian Greyhound is a sensitive and lively companion.

Regular scaling by a veterinarian is recommended (this applies to all toy breeds), but cream of tartar — mixed into a paste on a saucer with a little water, and applied with cotton wool — will often remove unsightly stains.

Feeding
About ½ can of a branded meaty product (376g, 13.3oz size), with biscuit added in equal part by volume; or 1-1½ cupfuls of a dry food, complete diet, mixed in the proportion of 1 cup of feed to ½ cup of hot or cold water.

Origin and history
This obedient and easy-to-train little dog is thought to originate from the Greyhounds depicted on the tombs of the Pharaohs. But it has existed in its present form for centuries and takes its name from its great popularity in 16th century Italy. It was favoured by Queen Victoria, who did much to popularize so many toy breeds during her long reign. Unfortunately for the breed, some English Toy Terrier blood was introduced in an effort to reduce the size further. This spoiled the breed character, and in an effort to restore it several dogs were imported from America. Alas, this did little to help matters and by the early 1950s only five registrations with the British Kennel Club remained. However, fresh stock was imported from Italy and, thanks to the determined efforts and dedication of breeders, the Italian Greyhound was once more firmly established as a stable breed by the early 1970s. 56▶

ENGLISH TOY TERRIER (Toy Manchester Terrier)

Good points
- Affectionate
- Easy to care for
- Good with children
- Intelligent
- Lively
- Good at expelling vermin

Take heed
- Tends to be a one-person dog that resents outsiders

The English Toy Terrier, which in the USA is called the Toy Manchester Terrier, is a most attractive, affectionate and game little dog, marvellously intuitive and loyal, but tending to attach itself to one person to the exclusion of others. It is usually healthy, easy to keep clean, odourless and an easy whelper if you wish to breed.

Size
The ideal weight is 2.7-3.6kg (6-8lb), and a height of 25-30cm (10-12in) at the shoulders is most desirable.

Exercise
Adapts well to town living provided adequate walks and off-the-lead runs are possible.

Grooming
A daily brushing will suffice. One of the advantages of this short-coated breed is that it does not shed. The coat can be massaged to effect a sheen; or equally beneficial is a weekly teaspoonful of cod liver oil in the food. Dry the coat with a towel after excursions on rainy days. Although the breed is robust it will, in common with most toy breeds, appreciate a warm coat in bitter weather.

Feeding
Recommended would be ⅓-½ can (376g, 13.3oz size) of a branded meaty product, with biscuit added in equal part by volume; or 1-1½ cups of a dry food, complete diet, mixed in the proportion of 1 cup of feed to ½ cup of hot or cold water. The owner may occasionally sub-stitute lightly cooked minced beef, mixed with biscuit. Lean meat scraps are appreciated. Water must be available to all breeds at all times.

Origin and history
(See also Manchester Terrier)
The English Toy is a smaller version of the Manchester Terrier, once a prodigious ratter and descended from the old Black and Tan Rough-haired Terrier. Their fitness owes something to the Italian Greyhound and the Whippet. The breed began in England under the name Toy Manchester Terrier, and was later known variously as Toy Black and Tan, and Miniature Black and Tan. They were recognized as English Toy Terriers (Black and Tan) by the British Kennel Club in 1962.56▶

Below: The elegant, compact and lively English Toy Terrier.

MINIATURE PINSCHER

Good points
- *Delightful hackney gait*
- *Easy to look after*
- *Fearless*
- *Good house dog*
- *Intelligent*
- *Rarely moults*
- *Suitable for town or country life*

Take heed
- *Do not overfeed*

The Miniature Pinscher (or Min Pin), sometimes called the 'King of the Toys', makes an ideal pet for the town dweller who, nonetheless, wants a lively sporting companion, not averse to an occasional day's rabbiting. It will follow a scent and give a good account of itself in obedience competitions. The breed's hackney gait is a delight to watch, as it trots along like a dainty little horse. It has the added advantages of rarely moulting and of requiring the minimum of attention to its coat.

Size
The height is 25-30cm (10-12in) at the withers. (There are some slight differences in the US standard as regards acceptable colour and size.)

Exercise
The Min Pin will exercise itself in a reasonable-sized garden or accompany its owner on a day-long trek. This adaptable dog will be happy living in a flat and being taken for walks around the park, or living a free country life.

Grooming
A daily brush and rub down with a chamois leather will keep the Min Pin gleaming.

Feeding
About ½ can of a branded meaty product (376g, 13.3oz size), with biscuit added in equal part by volume; or 1-1½ cupfuls of a dry food, complete diet, mixed in the proportion of 1 cup of feed to ½ cup of hot or cold water.

Above: The Miniature Pinscher is a neat, proud and alert toy dog.

Origin and history
The Miniature Pinscher is not a smaller version of the Dobermann Pinscher, but a much older breed descended from the German Smooth-haired Pinscher. It is suggested that the Italian Greyhound and the Dachshund contributed to its make-up. It achieved pedigree status by the Pinscher-Schnauzer Klub in 1895.

The Min Pin's tail is docked, and its cropped ears can be pricked or dropped. Indeed, were it not for these characteristics and colour variations, one might be forgiven for mistaking it at first glance for an English Toy Terrier. The Medium Pinscher, little known outside Germany, more closely resembles the Dobermann, with its wedge-shaped head and cropped ears. 56▶

GRIFFON
(Griffon Bruxellois, Griffon Brabançon. The Griffon Bruxellois is known in the USA as the Brussels Griffon)

Good points
- *Happy temperament*
- *Hardy*
- *Intelligent*
- *Long-lived*
- *Obedient*
- *Suitable for town or country living*

Take heed
- *No drawbacks known*

The Griffon is an attractive, happy little dog that makes a first-class family pet. It has an almost monkey-like face, with a knowing expression, and is hardy, intelligent and terrier-like in temperament. The breed, which is essentially Belgian, was originally used as a guard and catcher of vermin, particularly in stable yards. However, it took the fancy of royalty, thereby becoming a fashionable house pet.

There are two varieties, the Griffon Bruxellois and the Griffon Brabançon. The only difference is in the coat: the Bruxellois is a rough-coat, and the Brabançon a smooth-coat. Rough-coats and smooth-coats can appear in a single litter. The only variation in the breed standard is in the coat: roughs are harsh, wiry and free from curl, preferably with an under-coat; smooths are short and tight.

Size
Weight: 2.3-5kg (5-11lb), most desirable 2.7-4.5kg (6-10lb).

Exercise
Like most toy breeds it adapts well to town life and does not need a great deal of exercise, but a romp in the countryside will be greatly appreciated.

Grooming
The rough-coat needs twice yearly stripping: best to seek advice, or have this done professionally. The smooth-coat should be brushed, towelled, and gently rubbed down with the proverbial velvet glove or a piece of chamois leather. Watch with this and other small breeds that the nails do not grow too long. Purchase the proper nail clippers for the job from a pet store or pharmacy, and be particularly careful to cut down only to the 'quick'.

Feeding
About ½ can of a branded meaty product (376g, 13.3oz size), with biscuit added in equal part by volume; or 1-1½ cupfuls of a dry food, complete diet, mixed in the proportion of 1 cup of feed to ½ cup of hot or cold water.

Origin and history
The Griffon was first exhibited at the Brussels Exhibition in 1880 and is a truly Belgian breed. It seems likely that it derives from the Affenpinscher, to which it certainly bears a facial resemblance; the introduction of the Pug may be responsible for the Brabançon, or smooth-coat, which in the early days was not recognized.

An enthusiastic Griffon owner was the late Queen Astrid of the Belgians. Before World War I, the popularity of Griffons in their country of origin was immense, but the breeding programme was severely affected by the war.

Griffons have fortunately now found their way to most countries of the world, but showing differences exist. In its native land the Griffon is shown with cropped ears, a practice that is illegal in the United Kingdom, Scandinavia and Australia, and dependent on individual state law in the USA.56▶

LOWCHEN

Good points
- Affectionate
- Happy nature
- Intelligent
- Healthy
- Good show dog

Take heed
- No drawbacks known, except perhaps the need for skilful clipping

The Lowchen is a member of the Bichon family, sharing with the imperial Pekingese the title of little lion dog , because of the practice of clipping it in the traditional poodle exhibition cut, the lion clip, which, complete with mane and tufted tail, gives it the appearance of a lion in miniature. It is an affectionate, happy, healthy little dog, known in Europe for several centuries.

Size
Height: 25-33cm (10-13in) at the withers. Weight: 1.8-4.1kg (4-9lb).

Exercise
This breed adapts well to town or country; although usually presented more suitably for decoration than for sporting activity, it will enjoy regular walks in the park, or a run in the countryside. But many of the exotic breeds are

Below: Seemingly fragile, the Lowchen is robust and full of energy.

kept in breeding and exhibition kennels where, although extremely well looked after, they never have the chance of a muddy scamper.

Grooming
Clipping is best left to the expert, at any rate until a pattern has been studied and absorbed. Meanwhile, a daily brushing will keep the Lowchen looking handsome.

Feeding
Recommended would be $\frac{1}{3}$-$\frac{1}{2}$ can of a branded meaty product (376g, 13.3oz size), with biscuit added in equal part by volume; or 1-1$\frac{1}{2}$ cupfuls of a dry food. complete diet, mixed in the proportion of 1 cup of feed to $\frac{1}{2}$ cup of hot or cold water. Always ensure that the dog has an ample supply of water.

Origin and history
The Lowchen is thought to be a French dog. It is registered with the FCI as of native origin, under the title 'petit chien lion'. Certainly it was known in both France and Spain from the late 1500s, and is thought to have been favoured by the beautiful Duchess of Alba, for a dog bearing a strong similarity to the Lowchen appears in a portrait of that lady painted by the Spanish artist Francisco Goya (1746-1828). Probably the breed evolved in the Mediterranean area about the same time as the Maltese, the Bichon Frise and the Bichon Bolognese.
 The Lowchen is now a frequent contender in the show ring in many countries, but it has yet to become popular as a pet. 57 ▶

AFFENPINSCHER

Good points
- *Affectionate*
- *Intelligent*
- *Cute monkey-like appearance*
- *Excellent ratter despite small frame*
- *Good watchdog*

Take heed
- *Slow to make friends with strangers*

The Affenpinscher is an enchanting little breed, with an almost monkey-like appearance, whence the prefix 'Affen', which is the German word for monkey. In its country of origin it is often called the 'Zwergaffenpinscher' ('Zwerg' means dwarf). The French have dubbed it the 'moustached devil'. In any event it is an appealing, comical little dog, the smallest of the Schnauzers and Pinschers alert, gentle and affectionate, but always ready to defend.

Size
Height: 24-28cm (9½-11in).
Weight: 3-4.1kg (6½-9lb).

Exercise
Like most toy dogs it will be content with a walk around the park, but it will gladly walk you off your feet if that is your pleasure.

Grooming
Regular brushing will keep the Affenpinscher in good condition.

Feeding
Recommended would be ⅓-½ can of a branded meaty product (376g, 13.3oz size), with biscuit added in equal part by volume; or 1-1½ cupfuls of a dry food, complete diet, mixed in the proportion of 1 cup of feed to ½ cup of hot or cold water. When giving a dry feed, ensure that the dog has—as always—an ample supply of water.

Origin and history
Miniature Pinschers and Affenpinschers were, until 1896, classified as one breed. In that year, at

Above: The Affenpinscher's comical looks hide a sturdy watchdog.

the Berlin show, it was decided that the long-coated variety should be known as the Affenpinscher.

The Affenpinscher is an ancient German breed that was depicted by Jan van Eyck (1395-1441) and Albrecht Dürer (1471-1528). There is, however, some controversy as to its origin, though its nationality has never been in doubt. Some believe it to be related to the Brussels Griffon; others attribute the Brussels Griffon to the Affenpinscher; a third school of thought is that the Affenpinscher is a toy version of the German coarse-haired terrier, the Zwergschnauzer. In any event, this delightful breed was recognized by the American Kennel Club in 1936. It was introduced into the United Kingdom in 1975 and first shown at Crufts Dog Show in 1980. 57▶

BICHON FRISE (Bichon Bolognese)

Good points
- *Good pet*
- *Happy temperament*
- *Adaptable*
- *Intelligent*
- *Loves human company*
- *Attractive, lamb-like appearance*

Take heed
- *Requires meticulous grooming*

The Bichon Frise has been recognized by the British and American Kennel Clubs only over the past 10 years. It is a most appealing and happy little dog, which will surely become more popular when the public become acquainted with the breed.

Size
Height: less than 30cm (12in), smallness being highly desirable.

Exercise
Will enjoy a romp if you can bear to clean up that muddy coat afterwards! It will fit well into town living and regular walks, but will enjoy the occasional off-the-lead country run and a game in the garden.

Grooming
This is not the breed for novice exhibitors, or for those who are not prepared to spend time in meticulous grooming, bathing, trimming and scissoring. The effect, when complete, should be of an elegant white 'powder puff', the head and body trimmed to give a rounded effect, but showing the eyes. Hair around the feet should also be trimmed. Ask the breeder for a showing and grooming chart, and for a demonstration.

Feeding
Recommended would be ⅓-½ can of a branded meaty product (376g, 13.3oz size), with biscuit added in equal part by volume; or 1-1½ cupfuls of a dry food, complete diet, mixed in the proportion of 1 cup of feed to ½ cup of hot or cold water. Always ensure that the dog has ample water.

Origin and history
The Bichon, like the Caniche, is a descendant of the Barbet (water spaniel), from which the name Barbichon originates; later it was abbreviated to Bichon.

The little dogs are said to have originated in the Mediterranean area and were certainly introduced by sailors to the Canary Islands prior to the 14th century. There were then four varieties: the Bichon Ténériffe, the Bichon Maltaise, the Bichon Bolognese and the Bichon Havanais. The breed later found favour with the French and Spanish nobility and was included in paintings by Fran-cisco Goya (1746-1828).

A period of obscurity followed until, after World War I, soldiers took a few when they left France. A breed standard was written up in France in 1933, when the name 'Bichon à poil frise' (curly-coated Bichon) was adopted, and the word Ténériffe omitted from its title. Crufts Dog Show in London included a class for the Bichon Frise for the first time in 1980.

The Bichon Frise was first introduced into America in 1956, and from further imports a few years later breeding began in earnest. The breed was registered with the American Kennel Club in October 1972 and classified in the Non-Sporting Group of the AKC in April 1973.

The Bolognese is very similar to the Bichon Frise and is registered with the Fédération Cynologique Internationale) as an Italian breed. 57 ►

TOY POODLE

Good points
- *Affectionate*
- *Intelligent and long-lived*
- *Good sense of fun*

Take heed
- *Noisy if unchecked*
- *Not ideal as a child's pet*
- *Sensitive*
- *Suggest veterinary examination prior to purchase*

The Poodle has a character full of fun. It is intelligent and obedient. In the United Kingdom, it has proved a useful competitor in obedience competitions. It has a fondness for water, if the owner permits, but is much favoured for the show ring where, exhibited in the traditional lion clip, it is a beauty to behold. It is also, debatably, the most difficult breed to prepare for the ring, involving the handler in a day's canine beauty treatment.

Size
Height at shoulder should be under 28cm (11in).

Exercise
The Poodle will enjoy a ball game in the garden, practising obedience exercises or trotting beside you in the park.

Grooming
Use a wire-pin pneumatic brush and a wire-toothed metal comb for daily grooming. The lion clip is an essential for the show ring, but pet owners generally resort to the more natural lamb clip, with the hair a short uniform length. It is possible to clip your own dog with a pair of hairdressers' scissors. However, if, despite the help which is usually available from the breeder, you find the task tedious, there are numerous poodle parlours to which you should take your dog every six weeks. Regular bathing is essential.

Feeding
One third to ½ can (376g, 13.3oz size) of a branded, meaty product,

with biscuit added in equal part by volume; or 1-1½ cupfuls of a dry complete food, mixed in the proportion of 1 cup of feed to ½ cup of hot or cold water.

Health care
Fanciers will confirm that the Standard Poodle is the soundest of the varieties. It is possible to acquire healthy Toy and Miniature stock, but care should be taken to purchase from a breeder who puts quality ahead of daintiness. Watch out for signs of ear trouble, nervousness or joint malformations. Teeth need regular scaling.

Origin and history
The Poodle was originally a shaggy guard, a retriever and protector of sheep, with origins similar to the Irish Water Spaniel and, no doubt, a common ancestor in the French Barbet and Hungarian Water Hound.

The Poodle may not be, as many suppose, solely of French origin. It originated in Germany as a water retriever; even the word poodle comes from the German 'pudelnass' or puddle, and from this fairly large sturdy dog, the Standard Poodle, the Miniature and the Toy have evolved.

The breed has been known in England since Prince Rupert of the Rhine, in company with his Poodle, came to the aid of Charles I in battle. The breed was favoured also by Marie Antoinette who, rumour has it, invented the lion clip to match the uniform of her courtiers. It is also a popular breed in the United States. 57▶

PEKINGESE

Good points
- *Loyal and affectionate*
- *Brave guard dog*
- *Healthy and intelligent*

Take heed
- *Aloof, independent nature*
- *Subject to eye trouble*
- *Needs daily grooming*
- *Guard against exertion and overheating in warm weather*

'You have to say please to a Peke.' So said a well-known Pekingese breeder. Tell one off and it will sulk until you feel *you're* in the wrong!

The Pekingese likes to remind its owners of its regal background, and expects to be petted and pampered. It is not, however, a delicate creature; in fact, it is fearless and fun, and loves having toys to play with.

It is good with children, but comes into its own as an adult's sole companion, being the centre of attention and, preferably, having the run of the house. The restricted and neglected Peke is apt to become destructive through boredom. The Peke has a mind of its own and is condescending by nature. But when it decides to offer you its affection, you could not wish for a more loyal and loving companion.

Size
Dogs: 3.2-5kg (7-11lb). Bitches: 3.6-5.4kg (8-12lb).
There is not, as is often supposed, a miniature Pekingese, but within a litter may be found 'sleeve' specimens weighing no more than 2.7kg (6lb). Sleeve Pekes are so called because they could be concealed in the flowing sleeves of the Chinese mandarins.

Exercise
The Peke will happily trudge across fields with its owner, or be content with a sedate walk.

Grooming
The Pekingese needs daily brushing with a brush of soft bristles. The grooming of the underside is usually carried out with the Peke lying on its back, the rest of the job being tackled with the pet standing on a table, or on one's lap. Grooming a dog on a table is good preparation for a possible show career! It isn't necessary to bath a Peke frequently; as an alternative, talcum powder can be applied and brushed through the coat.

Feeding
The adult Pekingese thrives on about 170-227g (6-8oz) of meat supplemented by biscuits and the occasional non-splintery bone. Like most breeds, they appreciate vitamin tablets, which they will learn to beg for like sweets. An accessible water bowl is, of course, a 'must' for this and all breeds.

Origin and history
This regal little lion dog came to Europe following the Boxer Rebellion when, in 1860, the British invaded the Summer Palace in Peking and five Imperial Pekingese were looted from the women's apartments. Previous to this, it had been forbidden for anyone other than the Chinese royal family to own a Peke, and their theft was punishable by death.

One of the Pekes taken by the British was presented to Queen Victoria; it was appropriately named 'Looty', lived until 1872, and was the subject of a painting by Landseer. 59▶

TIBETAN SPANIEL

Good points
- *Confident*
- *Easy to train*
- *Happy nature*
- *Intelligent*
- *Good household pet*
- *Suitable for town or country*

Take heed
- *No drawbacks known*

The Tibetan Spaniel is an attractive small dog, with a happy, if independent, nature. It is easily trained and makes an ideal family pet, being reliable with children. In appearance it resembles a rather large Pekingese. It is also an enjoyable dog to show.

Size
Weight: 4-6.8kg (9-15lb) is ideal. Height about 25cm (10in).

Exercise
This dog requires average walks and off-the-lead runs.

Grooming
Needs daily brushing.

Feeding
Half to 1 can (376g, 13.3oz size) of a branded, meaty product, with biscuit added in equal part by volume; or 1½ cupfuls of a dry complete food, mixed in the proportion of 1 cup of feed to ½ cup of hot or cold water.

Origin and history
The Tibetan Spaniel was first discovered in the Tibetan monasteries where, to quote a reference in *Champion Dogs of the World* (G. Harrap, 1967), 'Reports indicate that it still turns the prayer-wheel of Tibetans who seek to reap the rewards of a devout life without the inconvenience of physical exertion'. However, this charming practice may have ceased since the Chinese takeover and outlawing of dogs. It is a close relative of the Tibetan Terrier and Lhasa Apso, both of which also originate from Tibet. The Tibetan Spaniel was first seen in England in 1905. 58▶

Below: Three beautiful Tibetan Spaniels.

CHINESE CRESTED DOG

Good points
- *No hairs on the carpet!*
- *Intelligent and devoted*
- *Good with children*

Take heed
- *Apt to be greedy*
- *Some folk find the reptilian skin unpleasant*
- *Can die of a broken heart if parted from its beloved owner*

The Chinese Crested has much to recommend it, as both pet and show dog. It is a handy size, clean, and odourless, and does not shed. It is dainty, alert, intelligent, courageous and gentle. It seldom requires veterinary aid and is a free whelper. It adjusts to cold or warm climates as its body temperature is 4°F (2.2°C) higher than that of humans; in fact, it has its own central heating system, the body feeling hotter to the touch after the animal has eaten. It has the ability to grip with its paws in a charming, almost human fashion.

A strange fact about the breed is that in almost every litter there are one or two haired pups, known as 'powder puffs'. Although these haired specimens have been excluded from selective breeding over a period of years, they are still apparent. Many people believe that the power puffs are nature's way of keeping the hairless pups warm. The powder puff dog is favoured by many fanciers and may now also be exhibited in the show ring.

Size
Ideal height for dogs 28-33 cm (11-13in) at withers. Ideal height for bitches 23-30 (9-12in) at withers. Weight varies but should not be over 5.5 kgs (12lb).

Exercise
The Chinese Crested is a lively little dog and enjoys a brisk walk. However, it happily works off a lot of surplus energy running after, and playing with, the chews and other toys that it so likes.

Grooming
The Chinese Crested needs frequent bathing, and the skin should be regularly rubbed with baby oil to prevent cracking and to keep it smooth to the touch. Care must be taken to prevent sunburn and to maintain the skin free of blackheads — to which they are prone in adolescence — and other blemishes. Facial hair and whiskers are usually removed before a show.

Feeding
Usually a rather greedy dog, this breed should nonetheless be content with ½-¾ can of branded dog food (376g, 13.3oz size) or the fresh meat equivalent, and a cupful of small dog biscuits. It is a good ideal to keep a bowl of biscuits accessible, so that the animal may help itself when peckish, but remove them if your pet becomes overweight.

Health care
These dogs lack premolar teeth, and thus it is inadvisable to give them bones. They are also allergic to wool.

Origin and history
Up until 1966, an elderly lady in the United States owned the only examples of the Chinese Crested in the world. Mrs Ruth Harris introduced four of these to the United Kingdom. Today the Chinese Crested is thriving, and classes for the breed are being included in an increasing number of dog shows. It is recognized by the British Kennel Club.

58▶

NORWICH TERRIER

Good points
- *Adaptable to most life-styles*
- *Equable temperament*
- *Fearless*
- *Good with children*
- *Hardy*
- *Lovable*

Take heed
- *No drawbacks known*

Prior to 1964 the Norwich Terrier and the Norfolk Terrier were recognized as one breed by the British Kennel Club. In 1964 the Norwich gained independent status as the prick-eared variety of the two. Its appearance and characteristics are otherwise identical with its Norfolk kin. In the USA both prick-eared and drop-eared varieties were known as the Norwich Terrier until 1 January 1979, when separate breeds were recognized.

The Official Standard states: 'A small, low, keen dog, compact and strong, with good substance and bone. Excessive trimming is not desirable. Honourable scars from fair wear and tear should not be penalized unduly.'

Size
Ideal height 25cm (10in) at the withers; this must not be attained by excessive length of leg.

Exercise
The Norwich Terrier will settle for regular walks if living in a town, but is happiest when allowed off-the-lead runs in the countryside. It is adept at ratting and rabbiting.

Grooming
Little grooming or trimming is required.

Feeding
Recommended would be ½-1 can of a branded meaty product (376g, 13.3oz size), with biscuit added in equal part by volume; or 1½ cups of a dry, complete food, mixed in the proportion of 1 cup of feed to ½ cup of hot or cold water. Increase rations if the terrier is in hard exercise.

Origin and history
There is controversy as to whether Colonel Vaughan of Ballybrick, Southern Ireland, or Mr Jodrell Hopkins, a horse dealer from Trumpington, Cambridgeshire England, deserves credit for founding the Norwich Terrier breed.

Colonel Vaughan hunted in the 1860s with a pack of small red terriers that had evolved from the Irish terrier. As there were many outcrosses, terriers with drop and prick ears came about, and breeders tended to crop the ears of the drop-eared animals until the practice became illegal. When it did, the Norwich Terrier Club protested loudly about the admittance of the drop-eared variety; when the breed was recognized by the Kennel Club, the Norwich Terrier Club requested that the standard should call for only those with prick ears.

Mr Jodrell Hopkins owned a bitch, a number of whose pups came into the hands of his employee, Frank Jones. Mr Jones crossed them with other terriers, including the Irish and the Glen of Imaal Terrier, using only small examples of these breeds; the progeny were known as 'Jones' or 'Trumpington' Terriers. There is a breeder who claims a direct line from Mr Jones' dogs to the Norwich of today.

The Norwich is a breed that has not been spoilt; for, perhaps surprisingly, it has—like the Norfolk—never gained great popularity. 59▶

KING CHARLES SPANIEL

Good points
- *Hardy, despite small stature*
- *Clean*
- *Loves children*
- *Usually gets on with other pets*

Take heed
- *Needs monthly bath*
- *Watch out for canker in ears*
- *Needs daily grooming*
- *Not suited to outdoor kennels*

The King Charles Spaniel (Black and Tan variety) is known in the USA as the English Toy Spaniel, the varieties of which are Prince Charles (tricolour), Ruby (red) and Blenheim (chestnut and white).

In 1903 an attempt was made in the United Kingdom to change the breed name to Toy Spaniel. However, the change was opposed by King Edward VII, a devotee of the breed, and it has retained the name, probably attributed to it because of Van Dyck's 17th-century paintings, which showed King Charles with these pets.

The King Charles is an ideal choice. It is a good mixer, marvellous with children and — despite its small stature — very hardy. It does, however, require daily grooming, regular bathing and, like the Pekingese, to have its eyes wiped every day; care must also be taken lest canker should develop in those well-concealed ears.

Size
The most desirable weight is 3.6-6.4kg (8-14lb).

Exercise
The King Charles will look forward to its daily outings, whether accompanying its owner on a shopping trip or going for a scamper in the park. It will be quick to learn how to carry its lead or a newspaper. Don't forget to rub it down with a towel after it has been out in the rain.

Grooming
Regular brushing with a bristle brush is essential. Examine paws for any trace of interdigital cysts, and ears for canker, often detectable by an unpleasant smell. Wipe eyes with cotton wool dipped in a weak saline solution to keep them clear of unsightly 'tear streaks'.

Feeding
About ½-1 can (376g, 13.3oz size) of a branded, meaty diet, with biscuit added in equal parts by volume; or, if a dry food, complete diet is used, 1½ cupfuls of feed mixed in the proportion of 1 cup of dry feed to ½ cupful of hot or cold water; or minced beef, lightly cooked, with biscuit added. Meat scraps are acceptable, as are canine chocolate drops as a reward or treat, but don't spoil those teeth by giving your dog cakes or sweet biscuits.

Origin and history
The King Charles is generally thought of as a British breed, but it can be traced back to Japan in 2000BC. The original breed was much in evidence at the English 16th-century court, when it closely resembled the present-day, longer-nosed Cavalier King Charles. As short-nosed dogs became fashionable, the King Charles Spaniel evolved.

The breed has many royal associations; one was found hidden in the folded gown of Mary, Queen of Scots, after her execution, and Macaulay, in his *History of England,* recalls how King Charles II endeared himself to his people by playing with these spaniels in St James's Park, 'before the dew was off the grass'. 60▶

CAVALIER KING CHARLES SPANIEL

Good points
- *Hardy, despite small stature*
- *Clean*
- *Loves children*
- *Usually gets on with other pets*

Take heed
- *Needs monthly bath*
- *Watch out for canker in ears*
- *Needs daily grooming*
- *Not suited to outdoor kennels*

Many people find it hard to distinguish between the King Charles and the Cavalier King Charles Spaniel; the Cavalier is larger, and there are marked differences in the head formation — the skull is almost flat between the ears and its stop is much shallower than that of the King Charles. However, it has the same characteristics of courage, hardiness and good nature, which makes it a suitable pet for any age group.

Size
Weight: 5.4-8.2kg (12-18lb). A small, well-balanced dog within these weights is desirable.

Exercise
Normal exercise requirements. Will adapt easily to town or country living. It should not, however, be kennelled out of doors.

Grooming
Regular brushing with a bristle brush is essential. Examine paws for any trace of interdigital cysts, and ears for canker, often detectable by an unpleasant smell. Wipe eyes with cotton wool dipped in a weak saline solution to keep them clear of unsightly 'tear streaks'.

Feeding
About ½-1 can (376g, 13.3oz size) of a branded, meaty diet, with biscuit added in equal parts by volume; or, if a dry food, complete diet is used, 1½ cupfuls of feed mixed in the proportion of 1 cup of dry feed to ½ cupful of hot or cold water; or minced beef, lightly cooked, with biscuit added.

Above: An attractive Cavalier King Charles pup.

Meat scraps are acceptable, as are canine chocolate drops as a reward or treat, but don't spoil those teeth by giving your dog cakes or sweet biscuits.

Origin and history
Reports by Pepys and other British diarists tell us that King Charles II spent more time playing with his 'toy spaniels' during Council meetings that he did dealing with matters of state. He even took his dogs into his bedchamber.

The Cavalier and the King Charles originate from common stock. When it became fashionable to produce a King Charles Spaniel with a short nose, the original type almost disappeared; but in the late 1920s, a group of breeders combined to bring back the old type of King Charles, prefixing its name with the word 'cavalier' to distinguish it from the newer, quite separate variety. 60▶

BORDER TERRIER

Good points
- *Good-natured*
- *Handy size*
- *Hardy*
- *Reliable*
- *Sporty working dog*
- *Unspoilt breed*
- *Fine guard dog*

Take heed
- *Needs space for exercise*

The Border Terrier is the smallest of the working terriers. It is a natural breed that evolved in the Border counties of England and Scotland, where its task was to worry foxes from their lair.
It is a hardy, unspoilt dog with an equable temperament, and usually gets on well with other animals.

Size
Weight: dog, 5.9-7kg (13-15½lb); bitch, 5.2-6.4kg (11½-14lb).

Exercise
The Border Terrier has immense vitality and is able to keep pace with a horse. It is unfair to keep one unless you can give it adequate exercise.

Grooming
The coat needs a little trimming to tidy up for the show ring, but other-wise requires the minimum of grooming.

Feeding
Recommended would be ½-1 can of a branded meaty product (376g, 13.3oz size), with biscuit added in equal part by volume; or 1½ cups of a dry, complete food diet, mixed in the proportion of 1 cup of feed to ½ cup of hot or cold water. Increase rations if the terrier is in hard exercise.

Origin and history
The Border Terrier was derived in the Border counties of England and Scotland in the middle of the 19th century, when it was the practice to produce a terrier tailor-made for the task it would perform. Sportsmen wanted a hardy dog able to run with hounds and bolt the fox from its lair.
   The Border Terrier, with its otter-like head, still works with hounds, and has been less changed to meet the dictates of the show ring than almost any other breed. It was recognized by the British Kennel Club in 1920. 61▶

Below: A Border Terrier with her pup.

AUSTRALIAN TERRIER

Good points
- *Courageous*
- *Devoted to children*
- *No human enemies*
- *Hardy*
- *Keen, alert watchdog*

Take heed
- *Has aggression of a natural ratter — watch out for the neighbour's cat!*

The Australian Terrier is a loyal and devoted dog, game, hardy, and utterly reliable with toddlers. It has no human enemies, but will give a good account of itself when called to do battle with other dogs. It is an exceptionally alert watchdog but, having given the alarm, is more likely to kill intruders with kindness. It makes an excellent companion, and its alertness and speed combine to make it an excellent ratter. The Aussie's coat is weather-resistant, so it can be kept either in the home or in an outdoor kennel.

Size
Average weight about 4.5-5kg (10-11lb) — in Australia, approximately 6.4kg (14lb). In both the United Kingdom and Australia, the desired height is approximately 25cm (10in) at the withers. (The desired UK weight seems to be changing in line with that recommended by the Australian Kennel Club.)

Exercise
This is an active and keen scenting dog with the skill and courage to hunt and attack food for itself. Nowadays it is rarely asked to use these abilities, but it should have the opportunity to unleash its energy with regular walks and off-the-lead scampers. Nonetheless, it will adapt to apartment living.

Grooming
Regular grooming with a bristle brush will stimulate the skin and encourage a good coat growth. If you are planning to show your Aussie, bath it at least a fortnight before the show; but during spring and summer, when show dates may be close together, don't bath on each occasion, as frequent washing will soften the coat.

Feeding
About ½-¾ can of a branded meaty product (376g, 13.3oz size), with biscuit added in equal part by volume; or 1½ cupfuls of a complete, dry food, mixed in the proportion of 1 cup of feed to ½ cup of hot or cold water.

Fat is an essential ingredient if you want the animal to have a healthy coat; so if the meat given in the daily ration is low in fat content, a teaspoonful of corn oil should be added to the daily feed.

Origin and history
The Australian Terrier was known by various names until 1889, the year in which a club was formed in Melbourne to foster the breed, which had been evolved from several varieties of British terriers brought to Australia by settlers.

The dogs of the settlers were all derived from British stock. Sporting types, capable of hunting and killing vermin, were highly prized. There was, however, the need for a small, game watchdog to guard the lonely homestead in isolated areas.

It is believed that the development of the purebred Australian Terrier derived from the progeny of a Yorkshire Terrier bitch smuggled in aboard a sailing ship in a lady's muff and mated to a dog resembling a Cairn Terrier. 61▶

CAIRN TERRIER

Good points
- *Intelligent*
- *Adaptable*
- *Hardy*
- *Lively disposition*
- *Can live indoors or out*
- *Family companion*

Take heed
- *A bundle of energy; needs the opportunity to release it*

The game little Cairn Terrier comes from Inverness in Scotland and, although a popular show dog elsewhere, and drawing large entries in terrier classes, it is still in Scotland that the Cairn really comes into its own as a family pet. Indeed, when I lived in a Scottish village during World War II, it seemed as if every villager was the proud possessor of a perky Cairn.

The Gaelic word 'cairn' means a heap of stones, and is therefore a most suitable name for a terrier that goes to ground. It is an affectionate, sporty little dog with an almost rain-resistant coat, very active, and rarely stubborn, and it makes an ideal family companion.

Size
Weight 6.4kg (14lb).

Exercise
The Cairn is an energetic dog and also an expert killer of rodents. It is in its element trotting with its owner across the fields, or playing a lively ball game with children. It will adapt to controlled walks on the lead and sedate town living, as long as it has a good-sized garden to romp in.

Grooming
The Cairn is an easy dog to groom or, indeed, to prepare for the show ring, as it is presented in a 'natural' condition. It should be brushed and combed, and have any excess feathering removed from behind the front legs and the tail. Any long hairs about the ears and on the underside should also be removed for tidiness.

Feeding
Small terriers do well on ¾ can of branded dog food (376g, 13.3oz size) or the fresh meat equivalent, supplemented with biscuits.

The Cairn is not a greedy dog and may prefer to have two small meals each day, rather than receiving its rations all in one go. It also enjoys the occasional large dog biscuit to chew.

A daily teaspoon of cod liver oil will keep the Cairn in good health.

Origin and history
It is on record that James VI of Scotland (James I of England) ordered from Edinburgh half a dozen 'earth dogs or terrieres' to be sent as a present to France and these, it is believed, were forerunners of the present-day Cairn, suggesting that more than 300 years ago a working terrier of this type was used for killing vermin in Scotland. Indeed, Mr J.W.H. Beynon in his work, *The Popular Cairn Terrier*, says that every Highland chieftain, in ancient days, had his pack of hounds and terriers, the latter being used to bolt the foxes, badgers and smaller fur-bearing vermin. He also writes that, as far as he could learn, the oldest known strain of Cairns is that founded by the late Captain MacLeod of Drynoch, Isle of Skye, which goes back over 150 years.

Mr John MacDonald, who for over 40 years was gamekeeper to the Macleod of Macleod, Denvegan Castle, kept this strain alive for many years, the Cairn then being known as a Short-haired Skye Terrier. 61▶

SCHIPPERKE

Good points
- *Affectionate*
- *Excellent guard*
- *Good with children*
- *Handy size*
- *Hardy*

Take heed
- *Not suitable for kennel life*
- *Needs affection and individual attention to thrive*

The Schipperke is a delightful breed that originated in Belgium, where its job was to guard canal barges when they had been tied up for the night. The name Schipperke is, in fact, Flemish for 'little captain'.

Apart from being an excellent guard dog, the Schipperke is a most affectionate animal, and particularly good with children. It is also hardy and long lived. However, it needs individual attention and likes to be treated as a member of the family; it also takes a while to accept strangers.

Size
The weight should be about 5.4-7.3kg (12-16lb).

Exercise
A Schipperke can walk up to 6 miles or more without any sign of fatigue; but it can manage with a great deal less exercise if its owner lives in a town.

Grooming
The Schipperke has a dense hard coat that needs very little regular grooming.

Feeding
Feeding is no problem: a Schipperke will eat anything that is offered to it, and one good meal a day, perhaps with biscuit at night, will suffice. Recommended for its size would be ½-1 can of a branded meaty product (376g, 13.3oz size), with biscuit added in equal part by volume; or 1½ cupfuls of a dry, complete food mixed in the pro-

portion of 1 cup of feed to ½ cup of hot or cold water.

Origin and history
The Schipperke originated in Belgium, but is often thought to be a Dutch dog, probably because Belgium and the Netherlands have been one country in the past. The breed is well over 100 years old; some claim it to be nearer 200 years old, but there are no records to support this theory.

How the breed evolved is subject to conjecture. Some classify it as a member of the Spitz family, others as the result of a terrier/Pomeranian cross. However, it seems likely that the Schipperke and the Groenendael have a common ancestor, the Schipperke closely resembling a smaller example of that other fine Belgian breed. 63▶

Below: The compact Schipperke is a lively companion for children.

LHASA APSO

Good points
- *Affectionate*
- *Confident*
- *Good with children*
- *Hardy*
- *Excellent show dog*
- *Suitable for town or country*

Take heed
- *Needs lots of grooming*
- *Not keen on strangers*

The Lhasa Apso, like the Tibetan Terrier and Tibetan Spaniel, comes from the mountains of Tibet. It is a shaggy little dog, rather like an Old English Sheepdog in miniature, and makes an excellent pet, the only possible drawback being its natural suspicion of strangers.

Size
Ideal height: 25cm (10in) for dogs; bitches slightly smaller.

Exercise
This lively breed needs plenty of walks and off-the-lead runs.

Grooming
Brushing and combing daily — and not for a few minutes only.

Below: The Lhasa Apso from Tibet is a solid, friendly and assertive dog.

Feeding
Half to 1 can (376g, 13.3oz size) of a branded, meaty product, with biscuit added in equal part by volume; or 1½ cupfuls of a dry, complete food, mixed in the proportion of 1 cup of feed to ½ cup of hot or cold water.

Origin and history
This is the dog that the Dalai Lama of Tibet offered to the Chinese emperors. It existed for centuries in the Tibetan mountains until brought to Europe, and elsewhere, by early explorers and missionaries. The words lhasa apso mean 'goat-like' and it was perhaps as guard and protector of the wild goats of Tibet that this glamorous breed of today first found favour. It was first seen at a European show in 1929. 61▶

SHIH TZU (Chrysanthemum Dog)

Good points
- *Affectionate*
- *Hardy*
- *Intelligent*
- *Loves children and animals*
- *Suitable for town or country*

Take heed
- *Best to tie back the topknot with a bow, or your pet could develop eye trouble*

Above: The affectionate Shih Tzu needs daily grooming for good looks.

The Shih Tzu is a happy and attractive little house-pet which adores human company and hates to be neglected. It is extremely intelligent, arrogant, and looks forward to the long, daily grooming sessions for which time must be allocated if you decide to buy this delightful breed.

Size
Weight 4.5-8.2kg (10-18lb); ideally 4.5-7.3kg (10-16lb). Height at the withers not more than 26.5cm (10½in).

Exercise
Short, regular walks, and off-the-lead runs.

Grooming
Daily brushing with a pure bristle brush. Do not neglect this task or combing out tangles will be painful. Keep the topknot from getting into the eyes and take care that the ears are free of matted hair.

Feeding
Half to 1 can (376g, 13.3oz size) of a branded, meaty product, with biscuit added in equal part by volume; or 1½ cupfuls of a dry, complete food mixed in the proportion of 1 cup of feed to ½ cup of hot or cold water.

Origin and history
The Lhasa Apso was highly prized by the Dalai Lama of Tibet who would habitually give prized specimens to emperors of China. It is likely that the Chinese may have crossed the Apso with the Pekingese to develop the Shih Tzu. As with the Imperial Pekingese, export of the Shih Tzu from China was forbidden, and it was not until the death of Empress Tzu-hsi in 1908 that the little shaggy dogs were smuggled out to Europe. 60▶

PUG

Good points
- *Happy disposition*
- *Good with children*
- *Intelligent*

Take heed
- *Over-feeding will result in a gross, short-lived dog*
- *Guard against vigorous exertion, bad ventilation and over-heating in warm weather*

The Pug is a gay little dog, which looks extremely elegant if not allowed to indulge its inherent greed. It makes a charming family pet, provided care is taken that it does not develop respiratory trouble through over-heating or vigorous exercise, for with its flat, squashed-looking face it can encounter similar breathing difficulties to the Bulldog.

Like the Bulldog, the Pug also has a tendency to snore. But it shares the foolhardiness of the Chihuahua and certain other toy breeds, in believing that attack is the best form of defence. A classic example is the death of the Empress Josephine's 'Fortune', the pampered beast that bit Napoleon on his mistress's wedding night, and met with an untimely end after an encounter with the cook's Bordelaise Bulldog.

Size
The weight should be 6.4-8.2kg (14-18lb).

Exercise
An energetic dog, the Pug will relish more exercise than many breeds of similar size. But remember that gluttony and a tendency to over-weight go hand in hand, as will fatness and lethergy if the animal's greed is undulged. The Pug will do best walking on the lead, and should not indulge in vigorous exercise for fear of respiratory trouble.

Grooming
A good daily brushing should be sufficient for good looks.

Feeding
About ½-¾ can of branded dog food (376g, 13.3oz size) or approximately 227g (8oz) of fresh meat daily, supplemented by dog biscuits. Some fanciers prefer to feed meat raw and this must be a matter of choice and, indeed, of the dog's preference. But remember that cooked meat is generally free of bacteria, and that guard dogs are often fed on raw meat to keep them on their mettle!

Origin and history
The Pug found its way to France with the Turkish Fleet in 1553. The little dogs were brought by the sailors as gifts for their ladies, and were subsequently known as 'Little Turks'. They also found favour in Holland, where the tinge of their coat was likened to the colour of the House of Orange. When William and Mary of Orange journeyed to Britain to ascend the throne in 1689, a number of Pugs accompanied them. For a period of almost 300 years the breed enjoyed a popularity similar to that of the Poodle today.

Alas, most Pugs were permitted to eat sweetmeats and other delicacies, and became so fat that they were regarded by many as an abomination. They gradually declined in numbers until in 1864 even Queen Victoria had difficulty in locating one to add to her kennels. However, some 20 years later the Pug Dog Club was formed and efforts were made to improve and standardize the breed, resulting in the elegant and solid little Pug we know today. 62▶

WEST HIGHLAND WHITE TERRIER

Good points
- *Attractive appearance*
- *Easy to train*
- *Gets on well with other dogs*
- *Good with children*
- *Handy size*
- *Suitable for town or country*

Take heed
- *No drawbacks known*

The West Highland White Terrier is a game, hardy little dog that originated in Argyle, Scotland. In recent years it has gained tremendous popularity because of its attractive appearance, sporting instincts and handy size. It gets on well with children and other dogs and makes the ideal family dog.

The West Highland White's coat is one of the breed's most striking features. It consists of a hard outer coat and soft under-coat.

Size
About 28cm (11in) at the withers. There is no weight standard for this dog in the United Kingdom or the United States.

Exercise
The Westie will adapt to town or country, and will live either indoors or in a kennel. However, it will be happiest as a family pet allowed to share the comfort of the fireside, but given adequate free runs in the countryside. Remember that it was originally used as a working terrier, and its job was to hunt fox and badger. It is also, of course, a good ratter. This breed will enjoy an energetic ball game.

Grooming
Although the Westie may be the ideal choice for someone who wants a healthy and active dog, it is perhaps not so ideal for the show aspirant who does not want to spend much time on grooming. The Westie's coat must be brushed and combed every day, and have surplus stripped twice a year. The neckline is particularly important, and straggly hairs should be removed from ears and tail. Ideally, the Westie's coat should be approximately 5cm (2in) in length, with the neck and throat hair shorter. It is probably wise to ask the breeder to demonstrate what is required before you make your purchase, and to let you have a grooming chart with full instructions. If you feel you cannot handle the task yourself, you can entrust it to a dog grooming parlour.

Feeding
One to 1½ cans (376g, 13.3oz size) of a branded meaty product with biscuit added in equal part by volume; or 3 cupfuls of a dry, complete food mixed in the proportion of 1 cup of feed to ½ cup of hot or cold water. The Westie loves burrowing in the earth, often retrieving a long-discarded, much-loved bone, so do let it have the occasional marrow or chop bone to get its teeth into — but no splintery bones, please.

Origin and history
The first West Highland White Terrier clubs were formed in 1905, when breeds such as the Cairn Terrier and Skye Terrier, which in the past had all been classified as Small Highland Working Terriers, attained individual status.

It does appear that in the late 1800s there existed a white Scottish Terrier, or Scottie, a strain of which was bred by Colonel Malcolm of Poltalloch, from which the name Poltalloch Terrier was derived; they were also known as Roseneath Terriers. 63▶

MANCHESTER TERRIER

Good points
- Alert and intelligent
- Clean
- Good family dog
- Great sporting companion
- Long-lived
- Suitable for town or country

Take heed
- Tends to be a one-person dog

The Manchester Terrier is an ideal choice for those seeking a small, hardy dog that causes no trouble and makes a great sporting companion. It will fit well into family life, but does tend to attach itself to one person.

It is long lived and seldom ill. It can live indoors or outside in a heated kennel, but will be happiest if given a place by the fireside.

Size
Desired height: dog 40.5cm (16in); bitch 38cm (15in). In America the Manchester Terrier is shown in two varieties: the Toy and the Standard. The Toy Variety (known elsewhere as the English Toy Terrier) has an upper weight limit of 5.4kg (12lb). The Standard Variety should be over 5.4kg (12lb) and under 10kg (22lb) in weight.

Exercise
The Manchester is in its element running free in the countryside. Town dwellers need not rule out this breed, however, if they can offer regular walks, off-the-lead runs and a garden.

Grooming
Manchesters do not like rain, despite its proverbial frequency in their place of origin, and should be rubbed with a towel if they get wet. Otherwise, a daily brushing will keep this essentially clean animal looking smart. Its coat condition is always an indication of health.

Feeding
Half to 1 can (376g, 13.3oz size) of a branded meaty product, with biscuit added in equal part by volume; or 1½ cupfuls of a complete, dry food, mixed in the proportion of 1 cup of feed to ½ cup of hot or cold water.

Origin and history
The Manchester Terrier can trace its lineage back to the old hunting 'Black and Tan' Terrier, which, in the north of England, had the reputation of rat killer supreme.

The Manchester Terrier — once closely related to a white English terrier that seems to have disappeared, probably because of its tendency to deafness — has evolved as a reliable household pet, retaining its sporting instincts while fitting happily into a home that requires an alert, lively pet. It is usually good with children.

At one time the Manchester Terrier and the English Toy Terrier were shown as Black and Tan Terriers with a weight division. The English Toy Terrier is now separately classified in England, but in the USA, where the Manchester Terrier is popular, breeding of toys and standards is permitted.

A number of Manchesters were exported from the United Kingdom to the United States, Canada and (later) Germany in the 1800s, and it is thought (see Dobermann Pinscher) that the Manchester aided the make-up of the Dobermann, certainly as far as its short, shiny black and tan coat was concerned. Earlier Manchesters had cropped ears, a practice that became illegal in the United Kingdom in 1895. 66▶

43

SMOOTH FOX TERRIER

Good points
- *Alert*
- *Intelligent*
- *Good family pet*
- *Second to none as a rat-catcher*
- *Smart appearance*
- *Useful medium size*

Take heed
- *Needs plenty of exercise*

The word terrier comes from the Latin word 'terra' meaning 'earth', the job of the terrier being to kill vermin and to worry or 'boot' the fox from its lair.

The Smooth Fox Terrier is arguably the smartest terrier bred for this purpose. It enjoyed almost unrivalled popularity just before and after the Second World War, and is always a popular contender in the show ring, though it has been said that the elegance of this terrier has been attained at the expense of its former hunting ability. It makes an ideal family pet.

Size
About 7.3-8.2kg (16-18lb) for a dog and 6.8-7.7kg (15-17lb) for a bitch in show condition are appropriate weights.

Exercise
The terrier once called 'the little athlete of the dog world' deserves a chance to live up to that title. It will adjust to a regular trot around the park — on a lead, of course — but deserves the opportunity for frequent off-the-lead runs, preferably in the country.

Grooming
Daily brushing with a stiff brush. Trimming is required a few weeks before a show, paying particular attention to the inside and outside of ears, jaw, and muzzle. Usually a chalk block is used to ensure that the coat is snowy white.

Feeding
Recommended would be ½ to 1 can of a branded, meaty product

Above: The Smooth Fox Terrier is a supreme working dog and makes an intelligent family pet.

(376g, 13.3oz size), with biscuit added in equal part by volume; or 1½ cupfuls of a dry, complete food, mixed in the proportion of 1 cup of feed to ½ cup of cold or hot water.

Origin and history
The Smooth-coated Fox Terrier has been around in its present form for at least 100 years. Before then, almost all terriers that went to earth were known simply as fox terriers.

It was in 1862 at the Birmingham, England, National Dog Show that the breed first made its debut in the show ring. Its ancestry probably came about through the terriers in the English counties of Cheshire and Shropshire, and also a hound variety, the Beagle. 65▶

WIRE FOX TERRIER

Good points
- *First-rate companion*
- *Good with children*
- *Intelligent*
- *Smart appearance*
- *Splendid ratter*
- *Trainable*

Take heed
- *Needs plenty of exercise*
- *Defends itself if provoked*

The Wire-haired Fox Terrier is, when well turned out, a delightful sight to see. It is intelligent, cheerful, and easily trained; a first-rate children's companion, with the typical terrier's 'get up and go'. Nowadays it is seen more frequently than the Smooth-coated variety.

Size
A full-size well-balanced dog should not exceed 39cm (15½in) at the withers – the bitch being slightly lower – nor should the length of back from withers to root of tail exceed 30cm (12in). Weight 8.2kg (18lb) in show condition, a bitch about 0.9kg (2lb) less, with a margin of 0.45g (1lb) either way.

Exercise
The Wire-haired Fox Terrier will enjoy nothing more than going rabbiting with its master. It adores sniffing out vermin and is not afraid of a fight, despite its usual good nature. It adapts well to life as a household pet, but really deserves a country home rather than apartment life.

Grooming
Hand stripping is required in spring, summer and autumn – more frequently if it is the intention to show. Normally a daily brushing will suffice, but watch the coat carefully as terriers are susceptible to eczema. Chalking is usual for a show.

Feeding
Recommended would be ½ to 1 can of a branded, meaty product (376g, 13.3oz size), with biscuit

Above: The Wire Fox Terrier is a popular show, working and pet dog.

added in equal part by volume; or 1½ cupfuls of a dry, complete food, mixed in the proportion of 1 cup of feed to ½ cup of cold or hot water.

Origin and history
The Wire-haired Fox Terrier is a separate breed from the Smooth-coat, although in conformation the breeds are the same. It undoubtedly derived from the wire-haired terriers around the British coalmining areas of Durham, Wales and Derbyshire, where it had existed for some time before gaining the attention of fanciers. It did not appear in the ring until 1872. It contributed to the development of the Kromfohrlander, a guarding and hunting breed little known outside its native Germany. 65▶

JACK RUSSELL TERRIER

Good points
- *Affectionate*
- *Handy size*
- *Sporty companion*
- *Full of character*
- *Adapts well to home life*

Take heed
- *Excitable in a pack*
- *Not yet a pedigreed breed*

The Jack Russell Terrier has become immensely popular in recent years. New owners often become incensed on finding that the breed they have sought and acquired cannot be registered with the British Kennel Club, for it is not as yet a pedigreed dog. The British Kennel Club is aware of efforts to standardize the breed, but unable to accept it while there is so much variation in colour, size and form.

Size
The Jack Russell Terrier Club of the United Kingdom has drawn up a provisional breed standard aiming to produce a uniform type of Jack Russell Terrier allowing for two different heights: 28-38cm (11-15in) at the shoulder, and under 28cm (11in) at the shoulder.

Exercise
The Jack Russell Terrier will adapt well to life as a household pet provided regular walks are given. However, it is really in its element in the countryside, ferreting, facing badgers or after foxes, for they are game little working dogs that like to be active. Packs of Jack Russells are kept at most hunt kennels.

Grooming
A daily brushing with a stiff brush.

Feeding
Recommended would be ½ to 1 can of a branded, meaty product (376g, 13.3oz size), with biscuit added in equal part by volume; or 1½ cupfuls of a dry, complete food,

mixed in the proportion of 1 cup of feed to ½ cup of cold or hot water. Increase the amont if the terrier is working.

Origin and history
Reverend Jack Russell, a sporting parson in Devonshire, England, who died almost 100 years ago, built up a strain of wire-haired fox terriers that would hunt with his hounds, go to ground and bolt the fox. The dogs were, in fact, hunt terriers. Jack Russell not only bred his unique hunt terriers but also judged terriers at West Country shows and was one of the earliest members of the Kennel Club. It could be that when the breed is established and proper records of pedigree are kept, we may yet see the Jack Russell listed with pedigreed dogs. Certainly the Jack Russell Terrier Club is working very hard towards achieving this aim. 65▶

Below: The Jack Russell Terrier, a sporty companion full of character.

LAKELAND TERRIER

Good points
- *Excellent with children*
- *Fine guard with strong warning bark*
- *Good family dog*
- *Handy medium size*
- *Sporty, but adapts well to home life*

Take heed
- *Might be too lively for the elderly*

The Lakeland Terrier is similar in appearance to the Welsh and Airedale Terriers. It makes a first-class family pet, being of sound temperament and convenient size, and is also a fine guard. It has been used in the past for both fox and badger hunting, but nowadays is kept mainly as a pet and has, in recent years, been a very successful contender in the show ring.

Size
The average weight of a dog is 7.7kg (17lb), bitch 6.8kg (15lb). The height should not exceed 37cm (14½in) at the shoulder.

Exercise
Unless they choose a toy breed, like the Yorkshire Terrier, nobody should choose a terrier unless they want a pet with plenty of zip. The Lakeland Terrier, true to its breed, is gay and fearless, always ready for a walk or a game. It is suitable for apartment living as long as its owner can provide regular exercise and, hopefully, those much loved days out in the country for off-the-lead runs.

Grooming
Trimming the Lakeland for the show ring requires some skill. Daily brushing will help keep the coat tidy but, even for a pet, professional stripping in spring, summer and autumn is recommended.

Feeding
Recommended would be ½-1 can of a branded, meaty product (376g, 13.3oz size), with biscuit added in equal part by volume; or

1½ cupfuls of a dry, complete food, mixed in the proportion of 1 cup of feed to ½ cup of cold or hot water.

Origin and history
The Lakeland Terrier originated in the Lake District of England, hence its name, but was originally known as the Patterdale Terrier after the place it was first worked with the local hunts. Although known as a working dog long before, the Lakeland did not make an appearance in the show ring until a Breed Club was formed in 1912. The breed was recognized in 1921 and well established by 1931. 64▶

Below: Lakeland Terriers are lively family pets.

WELSH TERRIER

Good points
- *Affectionate*
- *Bold*
- *Good temperament*
- *Great fun*
- *Handy size*
- *Obedient*
- *Good with children*

Take heed
- *No drawbacks known*

The Welsh Terrier has much in common with the Airedale, Irish and Lakeland Terriers and resembles a small Airedale in appearance. It makes a good household pet, generally has a good temperament, and is affectionate, obedient and great fun.

Size
The height at shoulder should not exceed 39.5cm (15½in). In working condition, 9-9.5kg (20-21lb) is a fair average weight.

Exercise
Regular daily walks and a romp in the garden will suffice, but like most terriers it will appreciate a run in wide open spaces. They were, after all, originally bred to run with a pack of hounds.

Grooming
The Welsh Terrier's coat needs stripping twice yearly and regular brushing to maintain it in show condition, but many pet owners resort to clipping their terriers. The coat is usually left on in winter to provide extra warmth.

Feeding
One to 1½ cans (376g, 13.3oz size) of a branded meaty product, with biscuit added in equal part by volume; or 3 cupfuls of a dry food; complete diet, mixed in the proportion of 1 cup of feed to ½ cup of hot or cold water.

Origin and history
The Welsh Terrier — like its close relation, the Irish Terrier — is of Celtic origin. In fact, two strains

Above: The compact Welsh Terrier adapts well to family life.

once existed side by side: that evolved by the Welsh from a purpose-bred Coarse-haired Black and Tan Terrier, and an English variety achieved through crossing the Airedale and the Fox Terrier. These two types caused much argument while recognition for the breed was being sought. However, the English variety appears to have died out, and the true Celtic strain was presented in 1885, the Welsh Terrier Club being founded a year later. The following year the Welsh Terrier was awarded championship status by the British Kennel Club. The first Welsh Terriers were taken to America in 1888, but not in any numbers until after 1901. 64▶

SEALYHAM TERRIER

Good points
- *Beautiful appearance*
- *Devoted*
- *Good with children*
- *Sporting*
- *Excellent show dog*

Take heed
- *Enjoys a scrap*
- *Needs lots of grooming*
- *Obstinate*

The Sealyham was bred as a rat and badger hunter but has evolved into an elegant pet and show dog for those with time to devote to its coiffure.

The popularity of the breed diminished after the Second World War, being overtaken by the West Highland White Terrier, for which it is occasionally mistaken although resemblance is slight, except in colour. Perhaps its depleted numbers were not a bad thing, as first class stock is now being produced.

The Sealyham is a game, lovable little terrier that becomes devoted to its owners and is reliable with children. However, it can be obstinate and snappy if not firmly, but kindly, disciplined when young.

Size
Weight: dog should not exceed 9kg (20lb); bitch should not exceed 8.2kg (18lb). Height should not exceed 30cm (12in) at the shoulder.

Exercise
This dog will adapt happily to regular walks around the park and off-the-lead runs. But give a Sealyham the chance and it will enjoy getting gloriously dirty scampering in the wet, muddy countryside.

Grooming
The Sealyham needs hand stripping at least twice a year, and daily combing with a wire comb to remove surplus hair. As mentioned elsewhere, stripping by the inexperienced can prove a disastrous experience for both owner and dog, so do have the job done professionally, or ask an expert to show you how. Clipping is excusable for the older dog, but will ruin the coat for showing.

Feeding
One can (376g, 13.3oz size) of a branded meaty product, with biscuit added in equal part by volume; or 1½ cupfuls of a dry food, complete diet, mixed in the proportion of 1 cup of feed to ½ cup of hot or cold water. And it will just love bones!

Origin and history
The Sealyham takes its name from Sealyham in Haverfordwest, Wales, UK, where the breed was created in the mid-1800s, using other terriers with proven ability as hunters of fox, badger and vermin. (Some say that the Sealyham owes its existence to a terrier imported into Wales from Belgium in the 15th century.) Haverford-west formed the first Sealyham Terrier Club in 1908, and Fred Lewis, founder of the Sealyham Terrier Club, is said to have done much to improve the strain. The breed was recognized by the British Kennel Club three years later. The American Kennel Club also recognized the breed in 1911.

The Sealyham has been very successful around the world as a show dog, particularly in America, where the breed made its show debut in California in September 1911. The American Sealyham Terrier Club was formed in 1913 to promote the breed both as a show dog and as a working terrier. 63▶

DANDIE DINMONT TERRIER

Good points
- *Courageous*
- *Intelligent*
- *Devoted to owner*
- *Keen sense of humour*
- *Excellent watchdog*

Take heed
- *Tends to be a one-person dog, whose friendship and respect must be earned*

Although once popular as a badger and fox hunter, the Dandie Dinmont is now kept mainly as a household pet: indeed, they fare better indoors as a single pet than living with their fellows in kennels. They do, however, tend to be a little suspicious of strangers, giving all their devotion to their owner. They are excellent guard dogs with a bark that should deter any burglar.

Size
The height should be 20-28cm (8-11in) at the top of the shoulder. Length from top of shoulder to root of tail should be not more than twice the dog's height, but preferably 2.5-5cm (1-2in) less. The ideal weight for a dog in good working condition is 8.2kg (18lb).

Below: The Dandie Dinmont will make a devoted pet and watchdog.

Exercise
The Dandie Dinmont is an adaptable dog and will be happy whether put to work killing foxes or enjoying the role of an old lady's pet. It would, however, be unfair to keep this active, inquisitive breed in a home without a garden.

Grooming
Grooming is not a difficult task, the only equipment needed being a stiff brush and comb. Old hairs should be removed with finger and thumb, allowing the under-coat to come through. Incidentally, don't use a trimming knife, because this will ruin the coat. Brush daily for good looks.

Feeding
Recommended would be ½-1 can of a branded meaty product (376g, 13.3oz size), with biscuit added in equal part by volume; or 1½ cupfuls of a dry, complete food mixed in the proportion of 1 cup of feed to ½ cup of water.

Origin and history
Most Dandies can be traced back to the late 1700s, to an individual named Piper Allan, something of a character of his day, who had two Dandie Dinmonts, called Charlie and Peachem. Also well known is James Davidson, who was renowned for his 'pepper and mustard' terriers, so called because of their colour: it was from Davidson that Sir Walter Scott acquired his dogs, and indeed it was from a character in his novel 'Guy Mannering' that the breed received its name. 65▶

SCOTTISH TERRIER

Good points
- *Straightforward and honest*
- *Reliable temperament*
- *Fine guard*
- *Utterly loyal*
- *Home-loving*

Take heed
- *Has little time for strangers; best for a childless couple or unattached owner*

The Scottish Terrier or Scottie has been aptly described as a gentleman. It is an honest dog, that will not look for trouble but on finding it it will always fight fairly. It is a devoted companion to its owner, but has little time for strangers and is not the most suitable of dogs for a family with children or a couple intending to add to their family. It will fight fox or badger, but enjoys itself just as much in an energetic ball game, and likes nothing better than carrying a stick or a ball in its mouth. Altogether an attractive and sporty little animal.

Size
Weight: 8.6-10,4kg (19-23lb).
Height: 25-28cm (10-11in).

Exercise
The Scottie loves nothing more than being out of doors and it would be wrong to deprive it of romps in the garden or regular walks several times a day. It can live happily either indoors or in an outside kennel, heated in winter.

Grooming
The Scottie needs daily brushing and combing, particularly its fine beard, and should be trimmed in spring and autumn.

Feeding
Recommended would be 1-1½ cans of a branded meaty product (376g, 13.3oz size), with biscuit added in equal part by volume; or 3 cupfuls of a dry, complete food, mixed in the proportion of 1 cup to ½ cup of hot or cold water.

Origin and history
The Scottish Terrier, once known as the Aberdeen Terrier, and generally known as the Scottie, has existed in various forms for many centuries, but it was not until after 1800 that line breeding began. The first Scottish Terrier Club was formed in Scotland in 1892, when a standard was laid down for the breed. 63▶

Below: The devoted Scottish Terrier makes a strong, sporty companion.

STANDARD DACHSHUND (and Miniature)

Good points
- *Affectionate*
- *Loyal family pet*
- *Sense of fun*
- *Watchdog with loud bark*

Smooth-haired

Take heed
- *Prone to disc trouble*
- *Self-willed*
- *Slightly aggressive with strangers, if unchecked*

The Dachshund (or Teckel) was bred as a badger hound in its native Germany. What was needed was a short-legged hound, with a keen sense of smell, coupled with courage and gameness; and a dog that could burrow — an ability that, if unchecked, today's Dachshund will demonstrate in your garden.

Some Dachshunds are still bred as hunting dogs and will bravely tackle an opponent larger than themselves, such as the badger. They would also defend their master until death. However, their role nowadays is mainly as a companion. They may be a little aggressive with strangers, if unchecked.

Size
Standard: Long-haired: middle weight up to 8.2kg (18lb) for dogs and 7.7kg (17lb) for bitches.

Miniature (long-haired, smooth-haired and wire-haired): Ideal weight 4.5kg (10lb). It is important that judges should not award a prize to any dog exceeding 5kg (11lb).

Smooth-haired: dogs should not exceed 11.3kg (25lb); bitches should not exceed 10.4kg (23lb). Wire-haired: dogs should weigh 9-10kg (20-22lb) and bitches 8.2-9kg (18-20lb).

Below: The Long-haired Dachshund's thick soft hair protects it against thorns, heat, cold and rain.

Long-haired

Wire-haired

Exercise

Regular exercise is important, as the tendency to put on weight must be discouraged. This does not mean you must take your pet on 10-mile treks, but short, frequent walks are advisable, with plenty of runs in a well-fenced garden.

Grooming

The Dachshund's coat is easy to keep in condition. The Smooth-coat needs only a few minutes' attention every day with a hound glove and soft cloth. A stiff-bristled brush and comb should be used on the Long-hair and the Wire-hair.

Health care

Disc trouble can befall the Dachshund because of its long back and stubby little legs. Anyone who has seen a young dog paralysed, while otherwise in good health, will recognize the need to keep their pet's weight within the breed standard and to prevent it from leaping on and off furniture. Treatment varies from injections of cortisone to an operation; some owners swear by an osteopath!

The Dachshund's teeth are prone to tartar. Regular scaling is recommended, but stains can be removed with a paste of water and cream of tartar, applied with a bit of cotton wool.

Feeding

Standard: Suggested would be ¾ can (376g, 13.3oz size) of a branded meaty product, with biscuit added in equal part by volume; or 1½ cupfuls of a dry food, complete diet, mixed in the proportion of 1 cup of feed to ½ cup of hot or cold water. A satisfactory menu for an adult may be based on 21g (¾oz) of food for each 454g (16oz) the dog weighs.
Miniature: ½ can (376g, 13.3oz size).

Origin and history

The Dachshund was bred as a badger hound, or hunting dog, and is known to have existed before the 16th century and to have been derived from the oldest breeds of German hunting dog, such as the Bibarhund.

When the German Dachshund Club was formed in 1888, there was only one variety, the Smooth-haired Dachshund, whose wrinkled paws, then a characteristic, have now been almost bred out. Today there are three varieties, with miniatures of each type: the Smooth-hair, Wire-hair and Long-hair. The Wire-hair was introduced through crossing with the Scottish, Dandie Dinmont and other terriers, the Long-hair by crossing the Smooth-hair with the spaniel and an old German gundog, the Stöberhund. The bandiness in the breed, due to a weakness in the tendons, has now been eradicated, as has exaggerated length.

In Europe during both World Wars, the Dachshund, recognized as the national dog of the Teutonic Empire, was often discarded, shouted at, or even stoned in the streets because of its German ancestry. Happily this sorry state of affairs has long since passed and the sporty, lovable Dachshund is again popular. 64▶

BEDLINGTON TERRIER

Good points
- *Adores children*
- *Always keeps its figure*
- *Good family pet*
- *Well behaved*
- *Good watchdog*
- *Easy to train*

Take heed
- *Could be dangerous in a pack*
- *Formidable fighter if provoked*

The Bedlington Terrier is an attractive, hardy little dog that resembles a shorn lamb in appearance.

It is a dog whose dainty appearance and love of children belies its first-rate watchdog qualities. It is also a breed that trains easily, and a number have been used successfully in obedience competitions.

The Breed Standard states: 'A graceful, lithe, muscular dog, with no sign of either weakness or coarseness. The expression in repose should be mild and gentle, though not shy or nervous. When roused, the eyes should sparkle and the dog look full of temper and courage.'

Size
Height should be about 40.5cm (16in) at the shoulder, allowing slight variation below in the case of a bitch and above in the case of a dog. Weight should be 8.2-10.4kg (18-23lb).

Exercise
The Bedlington, like most terriers, is a lively, inquisitive breed and will enjoy an off-the-lead run or energetic ball game. It will, however, adapt very happily to apartment life as long as it is given regular adequate walks.

Grooming
This breed's coat does not shed, which makes it a boon for the house-proud, the dead hairs staying in the coat until they are combed out.

The breed should be trimmed regularly (otherwise the coat will become tangly) and given a good brushing every day with a fairly stiff brush. Do not bath the animal too often or this may weaken its coat. Hair should be removed from inside the dog's ears fairly regularly, which can be done quite simply by pulling the hair with finger and thumb or tweezers.

Feeding
Recommended would be ¾-1 can of a branded meaty product (376g, 13.3oz size), with biscuit added in equal part by volume; or 1½ cupfuls of a dry food, complete diet, mixed in the proportion of 1 cup of feed to ½ cup of hot or cold water.

Origin and history
It is possible that the Greyhound or Whippet played some part in the origin of the Bedlington Terrier, and the soft topknot gives strength to the suggestion that it may share common ancestry with the Dandie Dinmont Terrier. Certainly a strain of similar terriers existed with tinkers in Rothbury Forest, Northumberland, in the 18th century, and in 1820 a Mr J. Howe came to Bedlington, Northumberland, with a bitch named Phoebe. This bitch was given to a man called Joseph Ainsley, who mated Phoebe to a dog named Old Piper, producing Young Piper, the first dog with the new name 'Bedlington' Terrier. From that time, 1825, systematic breeding of the Bedlington began. The breed was shown in the ring during the 1860s and the first Bedlington Terrier Club was formed in 1875. 62▶

Pomeranian 16▶

Papillon 15▶

Phalène 15▶

Smooth-coated
Chihuahua 14▶

Long-coated
Chihuahua 14▶

Yorkshire
Terrier 19▶

55

Maltese Terrier 20▶

Smooth Griffon
(Brabançon) 24▶

Rough Griffon
(Bruxellois) 24▶

English Toy
Terrier 22▶

Miniature
Pinscher 23▶

Italian Greyhound 21▶

Löwchen 25▶

Affenpinscher 26▶

Bichon Frise 27▶

Toy Poodle (English saddle, or lion clip) 28▶

57

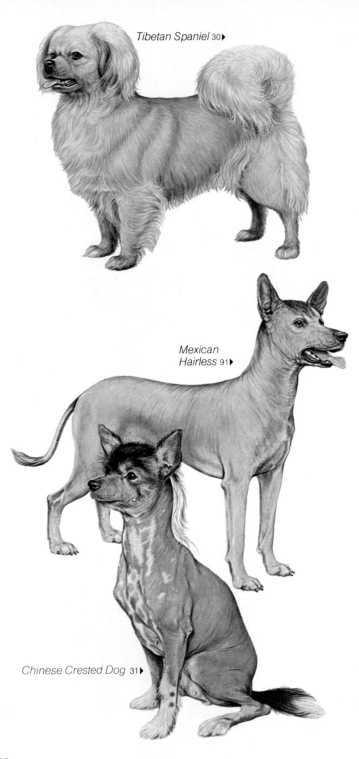

Tibetan Spaniel 30▶

Mexican
Hairless 91▶

Chinese Crested Dog 31▶

58

Pekingese 29▶

Norwich Terrier 32▶

Japanese Chin 17▶

King Charles Spaniel
(Tricolour) 33▶

King Charles
Spaniel (Ruby) 33▶

Cavalier King
Charles Spaniel
(Blenheim) 34▶

Shih Tzu 40▶

Lhasa Apso 39▶

Border Terrier 35▶

Australian
Terrier 36▶

Cairn Terrier 37▶

61

Bedlington Terrier 54▶

*Miniature Poodle
(Lamb clip)* 75▶

Pug 41▶

Irish Terrier 87▶

*Shetland
Sheepdog* 76▶

62

Schipperke 63▶

West Highland White Terrier 42▶

Scottish Terrier 51▶

Sealyham Terrier 49▶

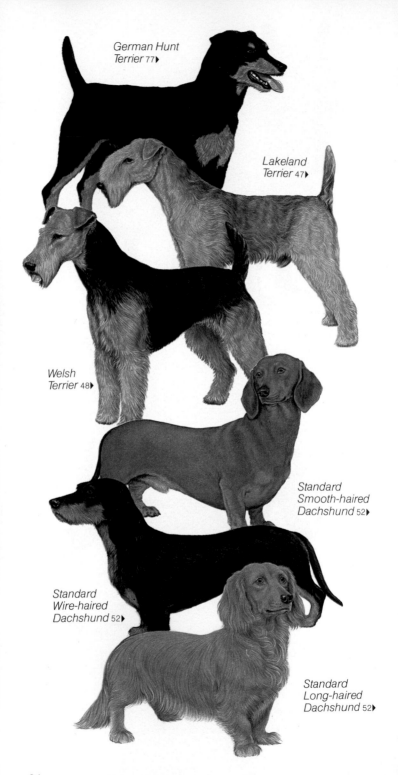

German Hunt
Terrier 77▶

Lakeland
Terrier 47▶

Welsh
Terrier 48▶

Standard
Smooth-haired
Dachshund 52▶

Standard
Wire-haired
Dachshund 52▶

Standard
Long-haired
Dachshund 52▶

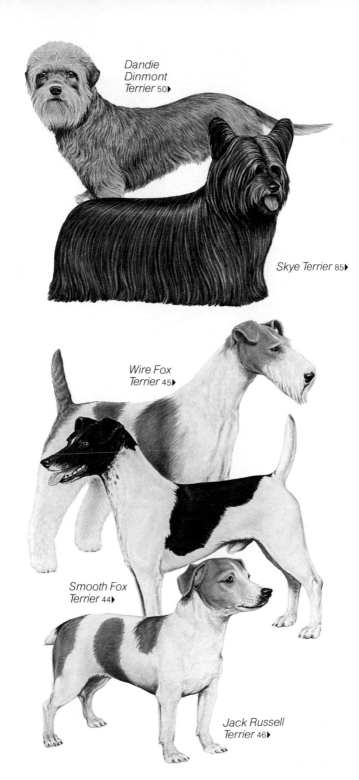

Dandie Dinmont Terrier 50▶

Skye Terrier 85▶

Wire Fox Terrier 45▶

Smooth Fox Terrier 44▶

Jack Russell Terrier 46▶

65

Miniature
Bull Terrier 97▶

French Bulldog 88▶

Boston Terrier 86▶

Tibetan
Terrier 78▶

Manchester
Terrier 43▶

Basenji 82▶

Beagle 79▶

Drever 80▶

Dachsbracke 80▶

Swedish
Vallhund 81▶

Pembroke
Welsh Corgi 83▶

Cardigan
Welsh Corgi 84▶

67

Bull Terrier 97▶

Staffordshire Bull Terrier 95▶

American Staffordshire Terrier 96▶

American Cocker Spaniel 89▶

English Cocker Spaniel 90▶

Finnish Spitz 93▶

Japanese Spitz 92▶

Standard Schnauzer 98▶

Hungarian Puli 94▶

Whippet 99▸

Australian Kelpie 100▸

Soft-coated Wheaten Terrier 102▸

Medium Pinscher 98▸

70

Kerry Blue Terrier 101▶

Border Collie 103▶

Brittany Spaniel 105▶

Welsh Springer Spaniel 71▶

Bruno de Jura
(Swiss Hunting Dog) 110▶

Lucernese
(Swiss Hunting
Dog) 110▶

Schweizer Laufhund
(Swiss Hunting
Dog) 110▶

Basset Griffon
Vendéen 109▶

Basset Artésien
Normand 109▶

Basset Hound 73▶

Lapphund 113▶

Norwegian Buhund 111▶

Keeshond 112▶

Pointing Wire-haired
Griffon 117▶

Portuguese Warren
Hound (Medio) 115▶

Portuguese Water Dog
(Long-coated variety) 116▶

MINIATURE POODLE

Good points
- *Affectionate*
- *Good sense of fun*
- *Intelligent and long-lived*

Take heed
- *Noisy if unchecked*
- *Not ideal as a child's pet*
- *Sensitive*
- *Best to have veterinary examination prior to purchase*

The Poodle has a character full of fun. It is intelligent, obedient and, in the United Kingdom, has proved a useful competitor in obedience competitions. It has a fondness for water, if the owner permits, but is much favoured for the show ring where, exhibited in the lion clip, it is a beauty to behold.

Size
Height at shoulder should be under 38cm (15in) but not under 28cm (11in).

Exercise
The Poodle will enjoy a ball game in the garden, practising obedience exercises or trotting beside you in the park. The miniature variety is a good choice for the apartment dweller.

Grooming
Use a wire-pin pneumatic brush and a wire-toothed metal comb for daily grooming. The lion clip is an essential for the show ring, but pet owners generally resort to the more natural lamb clip, with the hair a short uniform length. It is possible to clip your own dog with a pair of hairdressers' scissors. However, if, despite the help which usually is available from the breeder, you find the task tedious, there are numerous pet and poodle parlours to which you should take your dog every six weeks. Bath regularly.

Feeding
Recommended would be ¾-1 can of a branded meaty product (376g, 13.3oz size), with biscuit added in equal part by volume; or 1½ cupfuls of a dry food, complete diet, mixed in the proportion of 1 cup of feed to ½ cup of hot or cold water.

Health care
Fanciers will confirm that the Standard Poodle is the soundest of the varieties. It is possible to acquire healthy Toy and Miniature stock, but care should be taken to purchase from a breeder who puts quality ahead of daintiness. Watch out for signs of ear trouble, nervousness or joint malformations. Teeth need regular scaling.

Origin and history
The Poodle was originally a shaggy guard, a retriever and protector of sheep, with origins similar to the Irish Water Spaniel and, no doubt, a common ancestor in the French Barbet and Hungarian Water Hound.

The Poodle may not be, as many suppose, solely of French origin. It originated in Germany as a water retriever; even the word poodle comes from the German 'pudel-nass' or puddle, and from this fairly large sturdy dog, the Standard Poodle, the Miniature, and the Toy have evolved.

The breed has been known in England since Prince Rupert of the Rhine, in company with his poodle, came to the aid of Charles I in battle. The breed was favoured also by Marie Antoinette who, rumour has it, invented the lion clip by devising a style to match her courtiers' uniform. 62▶

SHETLAND SHEEPDOG

Good points
- *Beautiful*
- *Intelligent*
- *Faithful*
- *Ideal for competitive obedience*
- *Intuitive*

Take heed
- *Best kept in the home (not in a kennel)*
- *May be wary of strangers*

The Shetland Sheepdog is the perfect Rough Collie in miniature, a handy size for the owner who feels, perhaps, that the Rough Collie is too large for his home.

The Sheltie is a good family dog, but a little wary of strangers. It does not take kindly to being petted by those it does not know. It is faithful, supremely intelligent, and generally gives a good account of itself at training classes and in obedience competitions. It is good with horses, and a few are still used as sheepdogs.

Size
Ideal height measured at the withers 35.5cm (14in) for a bitch, 37cm (14½in) for a dog.

Exercise
Provided the Sheltie has a largish garden in which to expend its energy, and receives regular daily walks, it will be happy.

Grooming
Not so difficult to keep spick and span as might be believed. Brush regularly with a stiff-bristled brush and use a comb to avoid tangles, particularly behind the ears. Frequent bathing is unnecessary, but is advisable when the bitch loses her winter coat. The Sheltie is meticulous about its appearance and will often clean itself.

Feeding
One to 1½ cans (376g, 13.3oz size) of a branded meaty product, with biscuit added in equal part by volume; or 3 cupfuls of a dry food, complete diet, mixed in the pro-

Above: The Shetland Sheepdog, an obedient and faithful companion.

portion of 1 cup of feed to ½ cup of hot or cold water.

Origin and history
The Sheltie originated in the Shetland Islands off the north coast of Scotland, an area also famous for its tiny Shetland ponies, which, like the Shetland Sheepdog, have been bred with thick coats to protect them against the harsh climate.

The breed has bred true for some 125 years, but controversy at one time existed as to aims and requirements, the ideals of the club formed at Lerwick in 1908 conflicting with the desires of the Shetland Collie Club, whose desire was simply to produce a Collie in miniature. Both groups were similarly named. Luckily, agreement was reached in 1914 when the English Shetland Sheepdog Club was formed, and the Sheltie received separate classification by the Kennel Club. Today the breed's popularity is universal. 62▶

GERMAN HUNT TERRIER (Deutscher Jagdterrier)

Good points
- *First-class hunter, retriever and gundog*
- *Good traveller*
- *Robust*

Take heed
- *Needs a lot of exercise*
- *Somewhat aggressive*

The German Hunt Terrier is a popular breed in its country of origin. It is also well established in Austria and other German-speaking regions. It has yet, however, to be recognized by the English or American Kennel Clubs. It can be kept as a household pet, but is essentially a worker, needing plenty of exercise, and has a somewhat aggressive temperament.

Size
Weight: dog 8.8-10kg (19½-22lb); bitch 7.3-8.2kg (16-18lb). Height at the withers not more than 40.5cm (16in).

Exercise
Needs plenty of exercise. The German Hunt Terrier is a good car traveller and rarely suffers from sickness.

Grooming
Daily brushing is required.

Feeding
Half to 1 can (376g, 13.3oz size) of a branded, meaty product, with biscuit added in equal part by volume; or 1½ cupfuls of a dry, complete food, mixed in the proportion of 1 cup of feed to ½ cup of hot or cold water.

Origin and history
This is an essentially German breed derived from crossing the English Fox Terrier with the Lakeland and others, with a view to creating a hardy, dark-coated terrier. The first results were not encouraging although good working terriers were produced. However, by 1925, a satisfactory German Hunt Terrier had evolved that was able to go to earth and retrieve small game from land or water. It is a courageous dog willing to take on fox and boar as well as rats and small rodents, but has a somewhat aggressive terrier temperament.

The Association of the German Hunt Terrier has a list of work tests designed specifically for the breed. It accepts for breeding only Hunt Terriers that have achieved high pass marks. 64▶

Left: Bred in Germany as a working dog, the German Hunt Terrier can be kept as a pet but may be fierce.

TIBETAN TERRIER

Good points
- Charming 'shaggy' appearance
- Happy disposition
- Good house pet
- Weatherproof coat
- Popular show dog
- Effective watchdog
- Adaptable

Take heed
- No drawbacks known

The Tibetan Terrier is one of three small Tibetan breeds, the others being the Tibetan Spaniel and the Lhasa Apso, both of which are dealt with elsewhere. There is also a Tibetan Mastiff, which is a much larger breed.

The Tibetan Terrier, which in appearance resembles a small Old English Sheepdog, is in truth not a terrier at all, having no history of going to earth.

Size
Height at shoulders: dog should be 35.5-40.5cm (14-16in); bitches should be slightly smaller.

Exercise
The Tibetan Terrier enjoys an off-the-lead scamper and the freedom of a garden; otherwise normal, regular walks will suffice.

Grooming
Needs a thorough brushing every day to maintain smartness.

Feeding
Half to 1 can (376g, 13.3oz size) of a branded meaty product, with biscuit added in equal part by volume; or 1½ cupfuls of a complete, dry food, mixed in the proportion of 1 cup of feed to ½ cup of hot or cold water.

Origin and history
Bred in the monasteries of Tibet, with a history of all-purpose farm work, the Tibetan breeds first reached Europe at the beginning of this century, when both the Lhasa Apso and the Tibetan Terrier were referred to as Lhasa Terriers. The situation became somewhat confused, and in 1934 the British Kennel Club formed the Tibetan Breeds Association.

The Tibetan Terrier standard is included in the British Kennel Club's Utility group, and over the past 10 years the breed has attracted quite a number of enthusiasts. At the time of writing, however, the Tibetan Terrier has still to be recognized by the American Kennel Club. 66▶

Below: Not a true terrier, the Tibetan Terrier was bred for farm work in its native land. It is now increasing in popularity.

BEAGLE

Good points
- *Healthy*
- *Adores children*
- *Good with other pets*
- *Intelligent*
- *Merry and affectionate*
- *Good show dog*

Take heed
- *Will wander if gate is left ajar*
- *Will soon grow fat if given titbits*

The Beagle is a merry, affectionate little fellow, loving humans and other pets alike. The Beagle adores children and is a wonderful companion, equally ready for a romp or to lie by your feet on the hearthrug. This breed is equally at home in a small house or a mansion, and will guard its home and owner faithfully. It is not a barker, being mostly heard at the chase, in full cry. But, like most other hounds, it has the wanderlust, so care must be taken never to leave the garden gate ajar.

The Breed Standard states: 'A merry hound whose essential function is to hunt, primarily hare, by following a scent. Bold with great activity, stamina and determination. Alert, intelligent and of even temperament. A sturdy and compactly-built hound, conveying the impression of quality without coarseness.'

Size
It is desirable that height from ground to withers should neither exceed 40.5cm (16in) nor fall below 33cm (13in). In the United States there are two size varieties for showing purposes: below 33cm (13in), and over 33cm (13in) but not exceeding 38cm (15in).

Exercise
Exercise is no problem, because Beagles keep themselves fit as easily in a small garden as on a farm. But, like most dogs, they should be taken for a walk every day. They are notoriously healthy and robust, so you rarely need the services of a veterinarian.

Grooming
The short coat of the Beagle is tough and weatherproof, and needs no grooming. It is recommended that after a muddy walk the Beagle is left in its box for an hour to clean itself up.

Feeding
One meal a day is sufficient for a full-grown Beagle, with no titbits afterwards, as this is a breed that is inclined to put on weight. One to 1½ cans (376g, 13.3oz size) of a complete meaty diet, to which biscuit should be added in equal part by volume, is adequate; or 3 cupfuls of a dry food, complete diet, mixed in the proportion of 1 cup of feed to ½ cup of water.

Origin and history
The Beagle is one of the smallest of the hounds, embodying all their virtues in the least compass. An ancient breed, it has proved a joy to sportsmen for hundreds of years; Beagles were first mentioned by name in writings published in 1475. Followed on foot and on horseback, they have been hunted in packs after hare from time immemorial, and were first imported into the United States for this purpose.

Beagles are esteemed all over the world and have hunted many different quarries in varying climates, including jackal in the Sudan and Palestine, wild pig in Ceylon and deer in Scandinavia. In the USA and Canada they are used as gundogs to seek out and retrieve game, and to hunt by scent in competitive Field Trials. 67 ▶

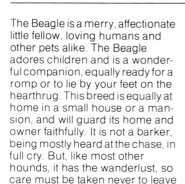

DREVER

Good points
- *Equable temperament*
- *Excellent nose*
- *Steady but slow worker*
- *Popular show dog in its native Sweden*
- *Good house pet*

Take heed
- *No drawbacks known*

The Drever is little known outside Scandinavia. It is, however, one of Sweden's most popular dogs.

It is a steady, though slow worker, and has a good nose for trekking fox, wild boar and roe deer, and will also drive them towards the gun. It has found favour in Scandinavia as a house pet. A similar dog, the Strellufs-stövare, is bred in Denmark.

Size
Height: dog 31.5-38cm (12½-15in); bitch 29-35.5cm (11½-14in).

Exercise
Needs plenty of exercise. Happiest when hunting.

Grooming
Normal daily brushing.

Feeding
One to 1½ cans (376g, 13.3oz size) of a branded, meaty product, with biscuit added in equal part by volume; or 3 cupfuls of a dry, complete food, mixed in the proportion of 1 cup of feed to ½ cup of hot or cold water.

Origin and history
The Drever is one of the most popular dogs in Sweden, a national breed said to have been derived from the mating of other Swedish hunting dogs with Dachshunds — there is something of the Dachshund and the Beagle in their appearance. At the beginning of the century, the breed was known by the German name of Dachsbracke. However, as it began to alter to meet Swedish requirements, the name was changed and recognition sought with the Swedish Kennel Club under the new name of Drever. This was achieved in 1949 and recognition by the FCI followed in 1953. This breed is not recognized by the British or American Kennel Clubs. It is a strong, muscular dog, bearing some resemblance to the Dachshund. Colours are red and white, yellow and white, or tri-colour. White must not predominate but must be apparent from all angles. These white patches on the Drever's coat help to make the dog more visible when it is being used to track down deer in the thick forests of its Swedish homeland. 67▶

DACHSBRACKE

The Dachsbracke is little known outside Germany. The breed is a close relative of the Swedish Drever and many authorities refer to the Dachsbracke and Drever as one. There are three varieties, the Westphalian, the Erz mountains and the Alpine; the former, the smallest of the three, is almost extinct.

The breed stands between 34 and 42cm (13½-16½in), has a short, dense coat and bears a passing resemblance to the Dachshund. A litter was bred in Britain in 1949. However, the Dachsbracke is not recognized by the British or American Kennel Clubs. It gained recognition in Germany in 1896. 67▶

SWEDISH VALLHUND (Västgötaspets)

Good points
- *Active*
- *Excellent drover/cattle dog*
- *Loyal*
- *Affectionate*
- *Intelligent*
- *Effective guard dog*

Take heed
- *No drawbacks known*

The Vallhund or Västgötaspets is a Swedish breed, similar in appearance to the Welsh Corgi. It is an active, intelligent worker and is rapidly gaining popularity in many parts of the world.

Size
Height: dog 33cm (13in), bitch 31.2cm (12.3in).

Exercise
Fares best if given plenty of exercise.

Grooming
Normal daily brushing.

Feeding
One to 1½ cans (376g, 13.3oz size) of a branded meaty product, with biscuit added in equal part by volume; or 3 cupfuls of a dry food, complete diet, mixed in the proportion of 1 cup of feed to ½ cup of hot or cold water.

Origin and history
The Västgötaspets, to give it its Swedish name, looks something like a Cardigan/Pembroke Corgi cross. There is certainly a connection between the Corgi and this attractive breed, but it is impossible to determine whether it evolved as the result of Vikings taking Corgis to Sweden, or if Swedish dogs brought to Britain developed the Corgi. It owes its present development to a Swedish breeder, Björn von Rosen. The Lappish Vallhund is similar, but it is a Finnish spitz used for herding. 67▶

Below: The Vallhund was developed in Sweden as a fine cattle dog.

BASENJI
(Zande Dog, Belgian Congo Dog, Congo Bush Dog, Bongo Terrier, Congo Terrier, Nyam-Nyam Terrier)

Good points
- *Adaptable to most climates*
- *Has no bark*
- *Gentle with children*
- *No 'doggie' smell*

Take heed
- *Does not like rain*
- *Bitches may come into season only once a year*
- *Mischievous*

The Basenji (the name is the translation of a native word meaning 'bush thing') is an interesting and attractive breed, its main claim to fame being that it has no bark. But only the bark is absent; the Basenji will growl and whine like other breeds, and can express itself feelingly with a distinctive chortle or yodel. The breed's vocal cords are present and it is believed that training, over thousands of years, to hunt game silently may account for their characteristic quietness.

The breed is well known for its gentle disposition and love of children, though it can be aloof with strangers. It has great curiosity and mischievousness.

Appealing features are its curling tail, high set and lying over to one side of the back, its habit of washing with its paw like a cat, and its forehead full of 'worried' wrinkles.

Size
Ideal height: dog 43cm (17in) at the shoulder; bitch 40.5cm (16in); but an inch either way should not penalize an otherwise well-balanced specimen. Ideal weight: dog 10.9kg (24lb); bitch 9.5kg (21lb).

Exercise
The Basenji is a great hunter and if not exercised has a tendency to put on weight. It is fleet-footed, tireless, and enjoys a daily walk and off-the-lead run. It is, incidentally, a breed that is particularly good with horses.

This is a breed that should not be kept in an outside kennel. It is essentially a house dog, which loves to stretch out in front of the fire, or to indulge in its strange habit of reclining in places off the ground. It is suitable for apartment living as long as it is given sufficient exercise.

Grooming
Regular use of a hound glove is recommended to keep the coat in good condition.

Feeding
About 1½-2 cans of branded dog food (376g, 13.3oz size), with an equal volume of biscuit, or 3 cupfuls of dry food, complete diet, mixed in the proportion of 1 cup of feed to ½ cup of hot or cold water; or ¼kg (½lb) of fresh meat, with biscuit. Green vegetables should be added to Basenji fare. They are also inveterate grass eaters and should have ample access to fresh grass.

Origin and history
Dogs of the Basenji type are depicted in many of the carvings in the tombs of the Pharaohs, and it is believed that these dogs were brought as precious gifts by travellers from the lower reaches of the Nile.

The Basenji almost disappeared from public view from Ancient Egyptian times until the mid-19th century, when it was discovered by explorers in the Congo and Southern Sudan.

The foundation stock recognized today derived from the Belgian Congo, with further imports from Sudan and Liberia. 66▶

PEMBROKE WELSH CORGI

Good points
- *Devoted companion*
- *Excellent guard*
- *Fond of children*
- *Hardy*
- *Tireless*

Take heed
- *Needs training when young — the inherent tendency to nip must be discouraged*

The Welsh Corgi (Pembroke) has, like the Cardigan, been worked in South Wales for many centuries, but has evolved as a popular and affectionate pet, particularly because it is a breed much favoured by the British royal family, whose pets have been known to take the occasional, much publicized nip!

Size
Weight: dog 9-10.9kg (20-24lb); bitch 8.2-10kg (18-22lb). Height: 25-30cm (10-12in) at the shoulder.

Exercise
Although traditionally a worker, the Pembroke adapts well to life as a domestic pet, with daily walks of average length. But beware: if you do not give sufficient exercise this breed will soon lose its figure!

Below: Daily exercise will keep the Pembroke Welsh Corgi looking trim.

Grooming
Daily brushing needed. The breed has a water-resistant coat.

Feeding
Give ½-1 can (376g, 13.3oz size) of a branded meaty product, with biscuit added in equal part by volume; or 1½ cupfuls of a dry food, complete diet, mixed in the proportion of 1 cup of feed to ½ cup of hot or cold water.

Origin and history
The Welsh Corgi (Pembroke) has worked in South Wales since the Domesday Book survey was instigated by William the Conqueror in the 11th century. Its traditional task was to control the movement of cattle by nipping at their ankles, and then getting quickly out of range. It has, however, a bolder temperament than the Cardigan.

Some say that the Pembroke derives from stock brought to Wales by Flemish weavers who settled in the locality and crossed their dogs with Welsh native stock; others point out the similarity that exists between the Welsh Corgi (Pembroke) and the Swedish Västgötaspets, suggesting that trading between the Welsh and the Swedes introduced the breed to Wales.

In any event, the Welsh Corgi (Pembroke) has been exhibited in Britain since 1925, receiving separate classification from the Welsh Corgi (Cardigan) in 1934. It is, perhaps, one of the best-known breeds in Britain, because of its association with Her Majesty Queen Elizabeth II. 67▶

CARDIGAN WELSH CORGI

Good points
- Devoted companion
- Excellent guard
- Fond of children
- Quieter temperament than the Pembroke

Take heed
- This breed had eye defects in the past, so seek a veterinarian's advice if necessary.

The Welsh Corgi (Cardigan) has been known and worked in South Wales for centuries. It is hardy, fond of children, and tireless, and, despite its original task of nipping the heels of cattle to bring them into line, has a more equable temperament than the Pembroke, and is less likely to nip the heels of unsuspecting visitors.

Size
Height as near as possible to 30cm (12in) at the shoulder. Weight: dog 10-11.8 kg (22-26lb); ditch 9-10.9kg (20-24lb).

Exercise
Although traditionally a worker, the Cardigan adapts well to life as a domestic pet, with daily walks of average length. But beware: if you do not give sufficient exercise this breed will soon lose its figure!

Grooming
Daily brushing needed. The breed has a water-resistant coat.

Feeding
Give ½-1 can (376g, 13.3oz size) of a branded meaty product, with biscuit added in equal part by volume; or 1½ cupfuls of a dry food, complete diet, mixed in the proportion of 1 cup of food to ½ cup of hot or cold water.

Health care
Avoid letting your pet jump from heights, especially if overweight; this could lead to painful spine trouble. The Cardigan is also prone to eye defects (progressive retinal atrophy); fortunately, these have now been almost eradicated from the breed.

Origin and history
The Welsh Corgi (Cardigan) has worked in South Wales since the Domesday Book survey was instigated by William the Conqueror in the 11th century. Its traditional task was to control the movement of cattle by nipping at their ankles, and then getting out of range.

The breed first made its appearance in the British show ring in 1925, classified as one breed with the Welsh Corgi (Pembroke); it received separate classification in 1934. Welsh folklore contains many references to this dependable, ancient breed, which has perhaps missed out on popularity due to the British royal family's particular fondness for its Pembrokeshire cousin. 67▶

Below: The Cardigan Welsh Corgi has a gentle temperament.

SKYE TERRIER

Good points
● *Beautiful in appearance*
● *Pleasant disposition*
● *Patient*
● *Devoted to its owner*

Take heed
● *Needs plenty of grooming*
● *Does not take kindly to strangers*

The Skye Terrier originated on the Isle of Skye in the Hebrides and is, despite its beautiful appearance, a relentless fighter if aroused. It is not a vicious dog, but tends to give total trust and devotion to its owner and has little time for strangers. Considerable care has to be given to the grooming of this breed. If given the chance they are valiant hunters, having been bred to hunt fox, otter and badger.

Size
Height 25cm (10in), total length 105cm (41½in), weight 11.3kg (25lb); bitch slightly smaller.

Exercise
It would be unfair to buy this gay little breed purely as a fashionable accessory, for they are tireless and enjoy nothing better than a long country walk and romp in fresh air.

Grooming
The Skye should be brushed daily and combed once a week with a wide-toothed comb. Incidentally, the coat does not reach its full beauty until the third year.

Feeding
Recommended would be 1-1½ cans of a branded meaty product (376g, 13.3oz size), with biscuit added in equal part by volume; or 3 cupfuls of a dry, complete food, mixed in the proportion of 1 cup of feed to ½ cup of hot or cold water.

Origin and history
The Skye Terrier is a legend — not only in Scotland, but throughout the world — because of the tale of

Above: Full of energy, the handsome Skye Terrier makes a devoted pet.

Greyfriars Bobby, whose statue stands near Greyfriars churchyard, Edinburgh. Following his master's death, Bobby would each day, for the next 14 years, visit the café that he had frequented with his master, where he would be given a bun, before retracing his steps to his master's grave, where he spent his days until his own death from old age, when the statue was erected in his memory.

The Skye evolved from the small earth dogs kept in Scotland to hunt foxes, badgers and other vermin. Although the Cairn and other breeds existed in the Highlands it would seem that the Skye owes its appearance to no-one, although the Highland terriers in early days were not separate breeds. 65▶

BOSTON TERRIER (Formerly American Bull Terrier)

Good points
- *Affectionate*
- *Excellent guard*
- *Good with children*
- *Rarely sheds coat*

Take heed
- *Not for outside kennelling*
- *Not the easiest type to breed and/or produce for showing*
- *Watch out for eye trouble*

The Boston Terrier is a lively and attractive American breed. It is intelligent and trainable, and makes a delightful companion, always ready for a walk or a game. However, achieving the desired markings can be a show aspirant's nightmare, and bitches frequently require caesarean section in whelping.

Size
Weight: not more than 11.3kg (25lb).

Exercise
This breed will happily settle for an on-the-lead walk, if you do not have a garden to offer it more freedom of movement. It is essentially a pet dog and should not be confined in an outside kennel.

Grooming
Daily brushing is needed. In the United States ears are cropped in some states according to state law. This practice is illegal in the United Kingdom. The coat rarely sheds.

Feeding
Half to 1 can (376g, 13.3oz size) of a branded, meaty product, with biscuit added in equal part by volume; or 1½ cupfuls of a dry, complete food mixed in the proportion of 1 cup of feed to ½ cup of hot or cold water.

Health care
The Boston is robust but, as in the case of the Pekingese and other round-eyed breeds, watch that dust and foreign bodies do not penetrate the eyes.

Origin and history
The Boston Terrier, sometimes called the 'American gentleman', can trace its ancestry from the mating of a crossbred Bulldog/terrier called Judge, imported to the United States from the United Kingdom in 1865. To later progeny were added a dash of English and Staffordshire Bull Terrier, until the dog we know today evolved. At first it was known as the American Bull Terrier, but as a result of objections from other Bull Terrier clubs it was renamed the Boston Terrier after the city responsible for its development. 66▶

Below: The Boston Terrier combines determination, strength and grace.

IRISH TERRIER

Good points
- *Alert*
- *Loyal protector*
- *Courageous*
- *Excellent ratter*
- *Good with children*
- *Trains easily*
- *Not as snappy as most terriers*

Take heed
- *Can be a prodigious fighter*

To describe the Irish Terrier as a dog that looks like a small Airedale with a self-coloured yellow coat would far from satisfy the many lovers of this ancient and most attractive breed. We have in the Irish Terrier a fine watchdog, a loyal protector and a most excellent family pet, the only drawback being its somewhat exaggerated reputation for fighting other dogs. True to its terrier blood it is tremendously courageous, and stories of faithfulness to its master are legion.

Size
The most desirable weight in show condition is: dog 12.3kg (27lb); bitch 11.3kg (25lb). Height at the shoulders should be approximately 46cm (18in).

Exercise
The Irish Terrier is a sporty little dog, which has been trained successfully to the gun and is first-class at destroying vermin. It has also been a creditable performer in obedience competitions. It will, however, adapt happily to life as a household pet provided it has a garden to romp in and is taken for walks and off-the-lead runs.

Grooming
Like the Airedale, the Irish Terrier will need hand stripping several times a year and it is best to have this done professionally — at least until you have learned the knack.

Feeding
Recommended would be 1-1½ cans of a branded meaty product (376g, 13.3oz size), with biscuit added in equal part by volume; or 3 cupfuls of a dry, complete food mixed in the proportion of 1 cup of feed to ½ cup of hot or cold water.

Origin and history
Irish sources say that the Irish Terrier was established in the country even before the arrival of their patron saint, St Patrick, some going so far as to say that the Irish Terrier is a smaller version of another of their national dogs, the Irish Wolfhound; but the relationship seems somewhat remote. It is more likely that the Irish Terrier is a descendant of the Black and Tan Wire-haired Terriers whose purpose was to hunt fox and destroy vermin in Britain some 200 years ago. Study of the Welsh and Lakeland Terriers will show the similarity between the breeds. It has a far larger following than the Glen of Imaal Terrier which originated from a valley of that name in County Wicklow, Ireland and is not often seen in the show ring. The Glen of Imaal Terrier is used as a working terrier to dispel foxes and badgers.

The standard breeding of the Irish Terrier did not take place until 1879 before which there was considerable variation of type, size and colour; it is said that the Irish Terrier in Antrim was black, brown and white, whereas those in Whitley were of a reddish colour and those in Kerry were black or black/brown. In 1879 a specialist Breed Club was formed, and in the following years the Irish Terrier in its present form and colour became tremendously popular. 62▶

FRENCH BULLDOG

Good points
● *Affectionate and devoted pet*
● *Loves human company*
● *Easy to train*
● *Adaptable*
● *Intelligent and alert*

Take heed
● *Lubricate facial creases with petroleum jelly to prevent soreness.*

The French Bulldog is a devoted animal and makes the ideal family pet. It has a keen, clownish sense of humour, is intelligent, and adapts well to town or country living. It is perhaps the healthiest of the Bulldogs and does not suffer from the over-developments or nasal difficulties of the Boston Terrier and the English Bulldog.

Size
The ideal weight is 12.7kg (28lb) for dogs and 10.9kg (24lb) for bitches.

Exercise
Short, regular walks. Do not over-exert in warm weather.

Grooming
Normal daily brushing and rub down with a silk handkerchief.

Feeding
One to 1½ cans (376g, 13.3oz size) of a branded meaty product, with biscuit added in equal part by volume; or 3 cupfuls of a dry food, complete diet, mixed in the proportion of 1 cup of feed to ½ cup of hot or cold water.

Origin and history
Credit must go to the French for the development of this breed. It is, however, uncertain whether it derives from small English Bulldogs taken to France by Nottingham laceworkers in the 19th century, or from crossings with dogs imported to France from Spain. In any event, this delightful breed is clearly the descendant of small Bulldogs, and by the beginning of this century it had found favour in both Britain and the United States. 66▶

Below: The charming French Bulldog excels as a friendly house pet and an obedient show dog.

AMERICAN COCKER SPANIEL

Good points
- *Adaptable to town or country living*
- *Beautiful*
- *Excellent family pet*
- *Intelligent*
- *Obedient*

Take heed
- *Needs lots of grooming*
- *Appreciates plenty of exercise*

The American Cocker Spaniel is an excellent hunter, and excels in flushing out and retrieving birds. It is also extremely popular as a household pet and is a beautiful, affectionate breed that will make an excellent companion in either town or country surroundings.

The Breed Standard states: 'The American Cocker Spaniel's sturdy body, powerful quarters and strong, well-boned legs show it to be a dog capable of considerable speed combined with great endurance. Above all it must be free and merry, sound and well balanced.'

Size
The ideal height at the withers for an adult dog is 38cm (15in), and for an adult bitch 35.5cm (14in). Height may vary 13mm (½in) above or below this ideal. A dog whose height exceeds 39.5cm (15½in), or a bitch whose height exceeds 37cm (14½in), or an adult bitch whose height is less than 34cm (13½in) should be penalized in the show ring.

Exercise
It must be remembered that the Cocker Spaniel was originally bred for hunting and, although it adapts happily to the role of companion and family pet, it will obviously fit in best with families who are prepared to give it two good walks a day and have a garden for it to romp in at its heart's content.

Grooming
The American Cocker, with its luxuriant coat, needs daily brushing and combing, and a bath and trim every 8-10 weeks. It is best to ask the breeder for advice, or to visit a professional dog groomer, because the skull and muzzle hair must be trimmed to precise accepted lengths with electric clippers, the neck and shoulders carefully scissored, and feathering left on the legs, ears and belly. Feet must also be trimmed. Obviously you may wish to attend to this ritual yourself, but it is advisable to be shown the procedure by an expert first.

Feeding
Recommended would be 1-1½ cans of a branded meaty product (376g, 13.3oz size) with biscuit added in equal part by volume; or 3 cupfuls of a dry food, complete diet, mixed in the proportion of 1 cup of feed to ½ cup of hot or cold water.

Origin and history
The American Cocker is smaller than the English Cocker, has a much thicker coat and, although originating from England, has been bred along different lines in the United States. Its elegant trousers and length of coat are the simplest means of clear identification.

An American Cocker was first shown in America at Manchester, New Hampshire, in September 1883, and when permission was given by the American Kennel Club for the two varieties to be shown, there was great enthusiasm for the American Cocker. 68▶

ENGLISH COCKER SPANIEL

Good points
- *Affectionate, gentle nature*
- *Excellent gundog*
- *Good with children*
- *Long lived*
- *Merry temperament*

Take heed
- *Overfeeding will cause weight problems*
- *Keep ears out of feed bowl*

The 'merry' Cocker, as it is called, makes an ideal family pet — a dog for Dad to take out shooting, or for the children to romp with in the garden. It is manageable, intelligent, and a good all-purpose gundog, second to none at flushing out game.

Size
The weight should be about 12.7-14.5kg (28-32lb). The height at the withers should be: dog 39.5-40.5cm (15½-16in); bitch 38-39.5cm (15-15½in).

Exercise
This is an active dog that needs regular exercise. It adores the country and is likely to return from a walk with tail wagging and covered with mud, so it is not perhaps the ideal choice for smart town dwellers; but it does enjoy home comforts, such as a place beside a warm fire.

Grooming
The Cocker requires daily brushing and combing, care being taken that its coat does not become matted. Particular care must be taken that the ears do not become tangled; and watch out that they do not flop into the feed bowl! You might consider taping them back while the dog is eating or using a special 'spaniel' bowl.

Feeding
Recommended would be 1-1½ cans of a branded meaty product (376g, 13.3oz size), with biscuit added in equal part by volume; or 3 cupfuls of a dry food. complete diet, mixed in the proportion of 1 cup of feed to ½ cup of hot or cold water. Obviously rations will need to be stepped up if the dog is taking vigorous exercise. This is a breed that will plead endearingly for titbits, which should be denied if the owner is to avoid an overweight or smelly pet.

With correct diet and exercise the Cocker Spaniel proves to be one of the healthiest and most long-lived of dogs. Its beautiful, appealing eyes make it difficult to refuse it anything, and there are few breeds in the world to challenge its beauty as a pup.

Origin and history
The Cocker Spaniel is particularly popular in Britain, and in the United States it is known as the English Cocker. It is also sometimes referred to as the 'merry' Cocker because of its happy, lively temperament and constantly wagging tail. Other titles bestowed upon it have been the Cocking Spaniel or Cocker, because of its one-time prowess at flushing out woodcock.

The Cocker Spaniel did however originate in Spain — whence the name 'spaniel' — and its ancestry can be traced back to the 14th century. It is believed to have been used in various countries in falconry. Today, however, it is in its element rabbit hunting. flushing out game for its master. The larger Field Spaniel is of a similar origin to the Cocker. It is a docile dog and a tireless worker, happily saved from extinction by a band of enthusiasts. 68▶

MEXICAN HAIRLESS (Xoloitzcuintli)

Good points
- *Even temperament*
- *Intelligent*
- *Affectionate*
- *No hairs on the carpet*
- *Pride of ownership — they are almost extinct*

Take heed
- *This breed must be kept warm*
- *Cries instead of barking*

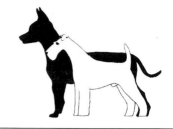

The Mexican Hairless Dog is one of the oldest breeds in the world, and in danger of becoming extinct. However, rumour has it that these animals are sometimes seen wandering along the waterfront in Hong Kong, and efforts are now being made to protect the breed in its native Mexico.

Unlike the Chinese Crested, this breed is totally hairless except for a tuft of short, coarse, and not very dense hair on the skull, though this should never be of the length or softness of the mane of the Chinese Crested. It is a quiet, rather reserved animal, growling only under provocation, and is similar in build to a Staffordshire Bull Terrier. It is described as gay and intelligent, yet at the same time dignified and unaggressive. Young pups tend to be snub-nosed and short-legged and do not conform to their adult appearance until late in their development.

The Mexican Kennel Club Standard states that the skin should be 'soft and smooth to the touch, particularly in those areas less exposed to the sun.'

Size
Weight 13.6-15.9kg (30-35lb). Height about 48cm (19in).

Feeding
Its normal diet is fruit and vegetables, but it can adapt to usual canine fare. This was proved when, some 20 years ago, two Mexican Hairless Dogs were quarantined in London Zoo. Recommended would be 1-1½ cans (376g, 13.3oz size) of a branded meaty product, with biscuit added in equal volume; or 3 cupfuls of a dry, complete diet mixed in the proportion of 1 cup of feed to ½ cup of water.

Health care
The Mexican Hairless sweats through its skin, unlike other breeds, which sweat through the tongue. They need a warm environment, with a heated kennel, and have a body temperature of 105°F (40.5°C) as against the normal canine temperature of 101.4°F (38.5°C).

Origin and history
The Mexican Hairless did not originate in Mexico, but was brought to that country by nomadic tribes of Indians from north-eastern Asia. It may even have come originally from as far away as Turkey, the land of the Turkish Toy Greyhound, another species of naked canine.

The little naked Xoloitzcuintli, as its new owners called it, was considered as a gift from the gods by the Aztecs, because when anyone was sick, the dog could warm the patient with its naked body.

The earliest inhabitants of Mexico, the Toltecs, had kept the blue Chihuahua in their temples for religious purposes. When the Aztecs conquered the Toltecs, dogs of both breeds were kept in luxury inside the temples. However, it is possible that the inevitable inter-breeding of the Mexican Hairless with the Chihuahua may have produced the Chinese Crested breed we know today. 58▶

JAPANESE SPITZ

Good points
- *Courageous*
- *Intelligent*
- *Loyal*
- *Lively*
- *Delightful show dog*
- *Good family pet*

Take heed
- *Tends to be a one-person dog*
- *Distrustful of strangers*

The Japanese Spitz is a close relation of the Norrbotten Spitz, but has developed as a separate breed in Japan, to which it was undoubtedly imported long ago. It has only recently come upon the international scene and is still comparatively rare.

Size
Height: dog, 30-40.5cm (12-16in); bitch, 25-35.5cm (10-14in).

Below: The charming Japanese Spitz, only just now becoming well known outside Japan, makes a rewarding show dog and reliable house pet.

Exercise
This dog is a natural herder, and enjoys its freedom. However, it adapts well to the life of a house pet, with regular walks.

Grooming
Normal daily brushing.

Feeding
One to 1½ cans (376g, 13.3oz size) of a branded meaty product, with biscuit added in equal part by volume; or 3 cupfuls of a dry food, complete diet, mixed in the proportion of 1 cup of feed to ½ cup of hot or cold water. 69▶

FINNISH SPITZ (Suomenpystykorva)

Good points
- *Beautiful*
- *Brave*
- *Excellent guard/housedog*
- *Faithful*
- *Good with children*
- *Home-loving*
- *Sociable*

Take heed
- *No drawbacks known*

The Finnish Spitz is Finland's national dog. It is popular in Scandinavia as both a hunter (mainly of birds) and a show dog. It also has devotees in Great Britain, where it is kept mainly as a pet and show dog. It is a beautiful animal with the habit of cleaning itself like a cat.

Size
Height: dog 44.5cm (17½in), bitch 39.5cm (15½in).

Exercise
This is a real outdoor dog, which likes to run free whenever possible. However, it also relishes its place by the fireside, so it should not be kept kennelled.

Health care
Although a hardy, healthy dog in adulthood, it can prove delicate as a pup, and this Spitz type is not the easiest to breed.

Grooming
Normal daily brushing.

Above: The lively Finnish Spitz makes an attractive guard dog.

Feeding
Recommended would be 1-1½ cans (376g, 13.3oz size) of a branded meaty product, with biscuit added in equal part by volume; or 3 cupfuls of a dry food, complete diet, mixed in the proportion of 1 cup of feed to ½ cup of hot or cold water.

Origin and history
Known for centuries in its own country prior to official recognition when the Finnish Kennel Club gained acceptance by the FCI. It originates from the Eastern zone of Finland and is mentioned in the country's epic the *Kalevala*.

Called the 'Finkie' by Lady Kitty Ritson, who pioneered the breed in Britain in the 1920s, it is related to the Russian Laika breed, a member of which was to orbit the Earth in an early space flight. It is a descendant of the earliest hunter dogs of Lapland and Scandinavia. 69▶

HUNGARIAN PULI (Puli; Hungarian Water Dog)

Good points
- *Easily trained*
- *Fine guard*
- *Highly intelligent*
- *Loyal*
- *Healthy*
- *Weather-resistant coat*
- *Adaptable*

Take heed
- *Tends to be a one-person dog*

The Hungarian Puli is a loyal, obedient dog, and perhaps the best-known of the Hungarian sheepdogs outside its homeland. It is easily distinguishable by its long, dark, corded coat, which is not so difficult to groom as might be believed.

Size
Height: dog 40.5-46cm (16-18in); bitch 35.5-40.5cm (14-16in). Weight: dog 13.1-15kg (29-33lb); bitch 10-13.1kg (22-29lb).

Exercise
Plenty of exercise is preferable, but this adaptable dog will fit in with city life, as long as it is at its owner's side.

Grooming
The coat hangs in long black cords, which in the adult dog reach to the ground, giving a tousled, unkempt look. The cords have to be separated by hand and regularly brushed and combed. Cleanliness is essential.

Feeding
One to 1½ cans (376g, 13.3oz size) of a branded meaty product, with biscuit added in equal part by volume; or 3 cupfuls of a dry food, complete diet, mixed in the proportion of 1 cup of feed to ½ cup of hot or cold water.

Origin and history
The Puli is better known than other Hungarian sheepdogs, such as the Pumi, the Komondor and the Kuvasz, probably because in its native land it directs the flock by jumping on or over the sheeps' backs. It is said to have existed for 1000 years, being a descendant of the sheepdogs brought to Hungary by the Magyars. It has proved itself as a fine water retriever, and has done well in obedience and police work. Hungarian shepherds favour their dark colour, which is easily picked out among the flock. 69▶

Below: The distinctive Hungarian Puli will make a loyal companion.

STAFFORDSHIRE BULL TERRIER

Good points
- *Excellent guard*
- *Fearless*
- *First-class ratter*
- *Good with children*
- *Very friendly to people*

Take heed
- *Needs discipline in youth*
- *Stubborn*
- *Liable to fight with dogs*

The Staffordshire Bull Terrier is a sound breed and excellent family dog derived from the crossing of a Bulldog with a terrier breed sometime in the 1800s. Probably the partner of the Old English Bulldog in this match was the Old English Black and Tan Terrier, which preceded the Manchester Terrier. It is, of course, an English breed, recognized by the British Kennel Club in 1935.

The Staffordshire Bull Terrier, in common with its close relation, the Bull Terrier, is a surprisingly gentle dog beneath a somewhat fearsome exterior. It is a good guard dog but adores its family and is utterly reliable with young children.

Size
Weight: dog 12.7-17.2kg (28-38lb); bitch 11-15.4kg (24-34lb). Height (at shoulder): 35.5-40.5cm (14-16in).

Exercise
The Staffordshire Bull Terrier can't resist a fight with another dog if given the chance, so keep this breed on the lead when walking on a public thoroughfare. It is a first-class ratter and a good companion in the field but will adapt to life in a normal-sized house and garden as long as regular walks are given.

Grooming
This breed requires little attention other than a good daily brushing.

Feeding
Recommended would be 1-1½ cans per day of a branded meaty

Above: The Staffordshire Bull Terrier is gentle with children.

product (376g, 13.3oz size), with biscuit added in equal part by volume; or 3 cupfuls of a dry, complete food mixed in the proportion of 1 cup of feed to ½ cup of hot or cold water.

Origin and history
The Staffordshire Bull Terrier has a bloody history, for it was evolved for the purpose of the once popular sport of bull and bear baiting, and later for dog fighting. Fortunately, however, with the banning of these sports the Staffordshire was developed as a companion dog and in the mid-1930s it was recognized by the Kennel Club as a pure breed, the standard being drawn up and a Breed Club formed in Cradley Heath, South Staffordshire. 68▶

AMERICAN STAFFORDSHIRE TERRIER

Good points
- *Affectionate*
- *Loyal to owner*
- *Excellent guard*
- *Fearless*
- *Skilful ratter*

Take heed
- *Needs discipline in youth*
- *Stubborn*

The American Staffordshire Terrier is not to be confused with the English Staffordshire Bull Terrier, which is a lighter dog with smaller bones. At one time the American Kennel Club was allowing the American Staffordshire Terrier to be shown with the Staffordshire Bull and, indeed, crossbreeding of the two was allowed. However, although the American Staffordshire's ancestry does originate in England, it has evolved as a quite independent breed.

Sadly, some of these dogs have, in recent years, been bred for the deplorable 'sport' of dog fighting. Everything possible is being done to eliminate this.

Size
Height and weight should be in proportion. A height of about 46-48cm (18-19in) at shoulders for the male and 43-46cm (17-18in) for the female.

Exercise
Appreciates plenty of exercise, but will adapt to town living if given long regular walks.

Grooming
This breed requires little attention other than a good daily brushing.

Feeding
Recommended would be 1-1½ cans per day of a branded meaty product (376g, 13.3oz size), with biscuit added in equal part by volume; or 3 cupfuls of a dry, complete food mixed in the proportion of 1 cup of feed to ½ cup of hot or cold water.

Above: With cropped ears, the American Staffordshire Terrier looks forbidding, but it makes a devoted pet as well as a fearless guard.

Origin and history
The American Staffordshire Terrier is of British origin derived from the traditional English Bulldog and an English terrier. The result was the Staffordshire Terrier, also known as the Pit Bull Terrier and later the Staffordshire Bull Terrier. Once it found its way to the United States, in 1870, it became known variously as a Pit Dog, Yankee Terrier and American Bull Terrier. The breed was recognized by the American Kennel Club in 1935 under the name of Staffordshire Terrier, which was revised on January 1, 1972, to American Staffordshire Terrier. 68▶

BULL TERRIER

Good points
- *Affectionate*
- *Excellent with children*
- *First-class guard*
- *Hardy*

Take heed
- *Best suited to country life*
- *Needs disciplining when young*
- *Powerful dog: you must be strong enough to hold lead!*

The Bull Terrier, despite its somewhat fierce appearance, is a gentle dog and utterly reliable with children, especially the bitch, which will literally let them climb all over her. However, if provoked by another dog, this terrier will happily fight to the death. The Bull Terrier never lets go! It is also a fine guard. It may let an intruder into your house, but one thing is certain: it won't let him out again!

Size
The standard has no height or weight limits: the Bull Terrier could be 31.75kg (70lb) or half that.

Exercise
The Bull Terrier is a powerful dog, with boundless energy, and should not be confined to apartment life, with a run in the back garden. More suitable would be a happily controlled country life with plenty of opportunity to run free.

Grooming
Normal daily brushing.

Feeding
If the dog is 9-22.7kg (20-50lb) give it 1-1½ cans (376g, 13.3oz size) of a branded meaty product, with biscuit added in equal part by volume; or 3 cupfuls of a dry food, complete diet, mixed in the proportion of 1 cup of feed to ½ cup of hot or cold water.

If it is 22.7-45.4kg (50-100lb) in weight, give 1½-2½ cans (376g, 13.3oz size) of a branded meaty product, with biscuit added in equal part by volume; or 5 cupfuls of a dry food, complete diet, mixed

in the proportion of 1 cup of feed to ½ cup of hot or cold water.

Health care
The Bull Terrier is a healthy dog. However, don't buy a white one without first checking that it can hear properly: white Bull Terriers are often born deaf.

Origin and history
This terrier began life as a fighting dog and battled on, seemingly impervious to pain, until bull baiting was outlawed by the British Parliament in 1835. Thereafter a dedicated band of fanciers determined to preserve the breed and refine it while preserving its strength and tenacity. They included James Hinks of Birmingham, England, who, by crossing the White English Terrier with the Bulldog and Dalmatian, produced a new strain of white dogs he called English Bull Terriers. Following the Second World War, coloured Bull Terriers made their appearance. However, the breed as a whole has never regained the tremendous popularity it enjoyed in the 1940s as companion and friend. Perhaps this is all to the good, as there are today few except first-class breeders producing sound, attractive stock, though a criticism has been that some animals are too whippety. 68▶

The Miniature Bull Terrier is a replica of its big brother the Bull Terrier in all respects except size. Height should not be more than 35.5cm (14in). Weight should be not more than 9kg (20lb) 66▶

STANDARD SCHNAUZER

Good points
- *Affectionate*
- *Lively and playful*
- *Good with children*
- *Intelligent*
- *Strong and healthy*
- *Excellent watchdog*

Take heed
- *Mistrustful of strangers*
- *Coat needs attention*

The Schnauzer is a good-natured, lively dog that loves both children and games. However, it does not trust strangers. There is also a miniature variety.

Size
Ideal height: bitch 46cm (18in); dog 48cm (19in). Any variation of more than 2.5cm (1in) in these heights should be penalized. Miniature: ideal height for the bitch is 33cm (13in) and for dogs 35.5cm (14in).

Exercise
Enjoys regular walks and ball games, but will adapt to country or apartment living.

Grooming
The Schnauzer should be brushed every day, and trimmed in spring and autumn.

Feeding
Recommended 1-1½ cans of a branded, meaty product (376g, 13.3oz size), with biscuit added in equal part by volume; or 3 cupfuls, of a dry, complete food, mixed in the proportion of 1 cup of feed to ½ cup of hot or cold water.
Miniature: ½ to 1 can of a branded, meaty product.

Origin and history
As the name implies, the Schnauzer is of German origin.
The breed originated in Bavaria and Württemberg where it was esteemed as a ratter and a cattle driver. However, when cattle driving died out, the breed found its way

to the city, where it gained popularity, coming to the attention of serious fanciers about 1900.
Schnauzers were first imported into America in 1905. The Schnauzer Club of America, formed in 1925, allows both the cropped and natural ear to be shown. 69▶

MEDIUM PINSCHER
(German Pinscher)

Good points
- *Alert guard*
- *Elegant appearance*
- *Lively pet*
- *Loyal to owner*

Take heed
- *Aggressive to strangers*
- *Fiery temperament*

The Medium Pinscher, previously known as the German Pinscher, is a very old breed, yet it is virtually unknown outside its homeland. This, the middle-sized of the Pinschers, bears far more similarity to the Dobermann than to the Miniature Pinscher and, like the Dobermann, has its ears cropped in its native country. The tail is docked and the coat is smooth and glossy. Colour usually black with small tan markings or self red. There is also a most attractive and distinctive harlequin Pinscher.
The Medium Pinscher was bred as a ratter, but nowadays is mainly kept as an alert, lively pet. Height is 40.5-48cm (16-19in). 70▶

WHIPPET

Good points
- *Clean*
- *Elegant*
- *Gentle and affectionate*
- *Good with children*
- *Fine show dog*
- *Excellent watchdog*

Take heed
- *Strong hunting instincts*
- *Needs plenty of exercise*

The Whippet is an excellent choice for those who want a dog that will combine the role of an affectionate and gentle pet with performance on the track and/or in the show ring. It has a peaceful temperament, but can be a little nervous in strange surroundings.

Size
The ideal height for dogs is 47cm (18½in) and for bitches 44.5cm (17½in). Judges should use their discretion and not unduly penalize an otherwise good specimen.

Exercise
The Whippet is a racer, capable of 56-64km (35-40 miles) an hour. It will adapt to life away from the excitement of a track, but make sure that you can give it plenty of vigorous exercise.

Below: Whippets make fine pets; they are clean, elegant and sporty.

Grooming
Generally, the Whippet needs little grooming, but the tail usually needs tidying up for a show. Teeth should be scaled regularly and the nails will need clipping.

Health care
Whippets are hardy, despite their delicate appearance, but should sleep indoors and be kept out of draughts.

Feeding
Recommended would be ½-1 can (376g, 13.3oz size) of a branded meaty product, with biscuit added in equal part by volume; or 1½ cupfuls of a dry food, complete diet, mixed in the proportion of 1 cup of feed to ½ cup of hot or cold water.

Origin and history
The Greyhound obviously had a hand in the Whippet's make-up, but there is some controversy as to whether the cross was with a terrier, a Pharaoh Hound or some other imported hound. The breed has been popular in Britain since the beginning of the century, and was exhibited at Crufts as early as 1897, being recognized by the British Kennel Club five years later. The Whippet is also popular in America, where the standard allows for a slightly larger dog. It was designed for racing and coursing, in which it excels. Many Whippet owners derive immense pleasure from keeping a dog that not only satisfies their sporting interests, but is also a popular show contender and a gentle, affectionate household pet. 70▶

AUSTRALIAN KELPIE / CATTLE DOG

Good points
- *Brave*
- *Equable temperament*
- *Excellent working dogs*
- *Good companions*
- *Loyal*
- *Full of stamina*
- *Intelligent*

Take heed
- *Need plenty of exercise*

The Australian Kelpie is a superb sheepdog descended from working imported Scottish stock. It is famed for the way it runs along the backs of sheep to reach the head of the flock. It is extremely fast and has an almost camel-like ability to go without water for lengthy periods. It is an attractive prick-eared dog with great intelligence and loyalty to its master.

The Australian Cattle Dog is an intelligent dog, amenable and first-rate at its job of driving cattle, sometimes covering vast distances. Like the Kelpie, it has an equable temperament and makes a loyal companion. Both these breeds are seen in the show ring in Australia.

Size
Kelpie. Weight: 13.6kg (30lb). Height: 46-51cm (18-20in) at the shoulder.
Cattle dog. Weight: 15.9kg (35lb). Height: 51cm (20in) at shoulder.

Exercise
The Australian Kelpie and the Australian Cattle Dog are accustomed to plenty of exercise.

Grooming
These breeds will benefit from regular vigorous brushing.

Feeding
One to 1½ cans (376g, 13.3oz size) of a branded meaty product, with biscuit added in equal part by volume; or 3 cupfuls of a dry food, complete diet, mixed in the proportion of 1 cup of feed to ½ cup of hot or cold water.

Above: Australian Cattle Dogs need lots of exercise.

Origin and history
The Kelpie derives from Collies brought to Australia by early settlers. Its ancestry can be traced to a pup named Caesar, later mated to a bitch named Kelpie, whose offspring included the famous King's Kelpie, winner of the first ever sheepdog trials in Australia in 1872. The Scottish writer Robert Louis Stevenson refers to the 'Water Kelpie' in his famous adventure story *Kidnapped*, giving credence to the suggestion that Kelpies derived from the working Scottish Collie.

The Australian Cattle Dog has emerged from crossings with the Old English Sheepdog (or Bobtail), Scottish Collies, Dingoes and Red Bobtails. 70▶

KERRY BLUE TERRIER (Irish Blue Terrier)

Good points
- *First-class guard*
- *Good sporting dog, but mainly kept as a pet*
- *Excellent with children*
- *Easy to train*
- *Coat does not shed*

Take heed
- *Loves a scrap, and not averse to starting one*

The Kerry Blue Terrier loves children and makes an ideal house pet. It does, however, have a fine Irish temper when aroused, and needs firm but gentle training when young if you don't want to be plagued with other folks' veterinary expenses.

Size
Weight: 15-16.8kg (33-37lb); greater tolerance in America.

Exercise
Bred as a working dog, it needs and deserves plenty of exercise.

Grooming
Daily brushing with a stiff brush and metal comb. You can easily learn to scissor trim the pet yourself. If you plan to show, however, there is a lot of work involved in show preparation.

Feeding
One to 1½ cans (376g, 13.3oz size) of a branded meaty product,

with biscuit added in equal part by volume; or 3 cupfuls of a dry food, complete diet, mixed in the proportion of 1 cup of feed to ½ cup of hot or cold water.

Origin and history
The Kerry Blue originates from the county of Kerry in south-western Ireland. The Irish Terrier had a hand in its make-up, to which the Bedlington Terrier and Bull Terrier are also said to have contributed.

The Kerry started life as a hunter of badgers and foxes, and has also done its share of otter hunting, being a keen, strong swimmer. It has guarded livestock and saw Army service during World War II. Now, however, it is predominantly kept as a popular pet and show dog. A Kerry Blue Terrier, Champion Callaghan of Leander, won the Best in Show award at Crufts in 1979. 71▶

Below: Properly trimmed, the Kerry Blue Terrier is a champion show dog.

SOFT-COATED WHEATEN TERRIER

Good points
- *Hardy*
- *Not finicky about food*
- *Intelligent*
- *Excellent guard*
- *Gentle with children*
- *Devoted to owner*

Take heed
- *A family dog, not suited to outdoor kennels*

The Soft-coated Wheaten Terrier is an exceptionally intelligent, medium-sized dog, which is defensive without being aggressive. It is an excellent house guard, but gentle with children. The Wheaten has strong sporting instincts, and some have been trained, with success, for the gun.

Size
Weight: dog approximately 15.9-20.5kg (35-45lb).
Height: dog approximately 46-49.5cm (18-19½in) measured at the withers; bitch slightly less.

Exercise
The Wheaten will relish plenty of exercise. It has excelled in the past as a hunter of rats, rabbits, otters and badgers, and will work any kind of covert, its soft coat being ample protection against the densest undergrowth.

Grooming
The Wheaten's coat does not shed. Daily combing should start from puppyhood, as regular grooming will keep the coat clean and tangle-free.

Fuzziness, not natural to the breed, can be aggravated by the use of a wire or plastic brush, and a medium-toothed metal comb should be used instead.

Bathing should be carried out as necessary; if showing, bathing the dog about three days before the event is recommended to avoid a fly-away appearance.

Ears, tail and feet need to be tidied, also any long, straggly hairs underneath the body.

Feeding
About 1-1½ cans (376g, 13.3oz size) of a branded meaty product with biscuit added in equal part by volume, or 3 cupfuls of a complete dry food, mixed in the proportion of 1 cup of feed to ½ cup of hot or cold water. Meat scraps and non-splintery bones are acceptable.

Origin and history
The origin of the Soft-coated Wheaten, like that of so many breeds, has been lost in the mists of antiquity. However, from old pictures and records, the breed has been traced back at least 200 years in Ireland, where for many generations there was hardly a farm or smallholding that did not boast an attendant Wheaten that was valued for its sterling qualities.

It is recorded that the Soft-coated Wheaten Terrier is the oldest Irish breed of terrier, said to be the progenitor of the Kerry Blue and Irish Terrier. Legend tells us that a blue dog swam ashore from a ship wrecked in Tralee Bay about 180 years ago. This dog mated the native Wheaten and from this originated the Kerry Blue. Wheaten-coloured pups have appeared in Kerry Blue litters from time to time. There is no record of cross-breeding in the Wheaten and it appears today to be much as it always has been.

The breed was recognized by the Irish Kennel Club in 1937 and first registered in Britain in 1971. Although reaching America in 1946, the breed was not given show classification until 1973. 70▶

BORDER COLLIE

Good points
- Intelligent
- Loyal
- Ideal choice for obedience competitions
- Good family or working dog

Take heed
- This breed will herd anything, people included, if sheep and cattle are not available

The Border Collie is a first-class, everyday working dog, famed for herding cattle and rounding up sheep. This is the star of sheepdog trials, the persistent winner of obedience competitions, the breed favoured by those who want a 'working' dog.

The Border Collie (the name refers to the English-Scottish border) was bred for speed, stamina and brains. It makes a first-class companion, is good with children, and is one of the most trainable dogs.

Size
Dog about 53cm (21in); bitch slightly less.

Exercise
This is essentially a working dog that enjoys being out of doors, whether trotting at its master's heels on a routine walk, doing exercises at a dog training class, or working on a farm. It will adapt to whatever role you have for it, but is not ideally suited to town life.

Grooming
Brush regularly with a good pony dandy brush and comb. Inspect the ears for signs of canker, and the ears and feet for foreign matter. Dead fur should be removed when grooming.

Feeding
About 1-1½ cans (376g, 13.3oz size) of a branded meaty product with biscuit added in equal part by volume, or 3 cupfuls of a complete dry food, mixed in the proportion of 1 cup of feed to ½ cup of

Above: The Border Collie is essentially a working dog.

hot or cold water. Meat scraps and non-splintery bones are acceptable.

Origin and history
The present-day Border Collie is a modern strain descended from Collies of the Lowland and Border counties of England and Scotland. They are working sheepdogs of a distinct, recognizable type, which have been exported to many countries of the world where sheep are farmed, and they are also excellent as guide dogs for the blind.

It was not until July 1976 that a standard for the breed was approved by the British Kennel Club from a combination of several proposed standards submitted to them by interested bodies, including the recognized one from the Australian KC. 71▶

STABYHOUN

Good points
- *Affectionate*
- *Easily trained*
- *Excellent guard dog*
- *Fine all-purpose sporting dog*
- *Hardy*
- *Has great stamina*
- *Good with children*

Take heed
- *No drawbacks known*

The Stabyhoun is one of the most popular dogs in its native Holland, but is little known elsewhere.

This is an excellent all-purpose sporting dog, nowadays kept mainly as a companion house dog. It is reliable with children, has an affectionate nature, is easily trained, and has an equable temperament. It is a splendid retriever, with a good nose.

Size
Dog up to 49.5cm (19½in) at the withers, bitch somewhat smaller.

Exercise
The Stabyhoun excels at working in the field as a retriever, doing the job for which it was bred. It adapts well to town life as long as it has ample opportunity to run free.

Below: The sturdy Stabyhoun is a popular retriever in Holland.

Grooming
Regular brushing will keep the coat in good condition.

Feeding
About 1-1½ cans (376g, 13.3oz size) of a branded meaty product with biscuit added in equal part by volume, or 3 cupfuls of a complete dry food, mixed in the proportion of 1 cup of feed to ½ cup of hot or cold water. Meat scraps and non-splintery bones are acceptable.

Origin and history
The Stabyhoun was recognized by the Dutch Kennel Club in 1942, but it has existed in the Netherlands since as long ago as 1800, when it was bred in the Friesland district as an all-purpose gundog, but primarily as a dispeller of vermin. Crossed with the Wetterhoun it made a formidable ratter!

BRITTANY SPANIEL

Good points
- *Affectionate*
- *Intelligent*
- *Excellent pointer*
- *Good nose*
- *Tireless*
- *Loyal*

Take heed
- *A devoted, sensitive dog that needs kind handling*

The Brittany Spaniel combines well the roles of hunter and companion. It has a natural talent for pointing and has been described as more like a setter than a spaniel. It has an excellent nose, and can cope with difficult terrain. It is, however, a sensitive animal that expects, and deserves, every consideration from its master. It is easily distinguishable by its short, stumpy tail. This breed is relatively unknown in the United Kingdom, but has been successful in Field Trials in the USA.

Size
Height: maximum 52cm (20½in), minimum 46.5cm (18¼in); ideal for dog 49-51cm (19¼-20in), for bitch 47.5-50cm (18¾-19¾in).

Exercise
Relishes plenty of exercise.

Grooming
Daily brushing. Take care that ears, eyes and paws are clean.

Feeding
One to 1½ cans (376g, 13.3oz size) of a branded meaty product, with biscuit added in equal part by volume; or 3 cupfuls of a dry food, complete diet, mixed in the proportion of 1 cup of feed to ½ cup of hot or cold water.

Origin and history
The Brittany probably originated either in Spain or in the Argoat Forests of Brittany. There is also a story that one of the red and white English Setters of a Breton count mated with a Breton bitch, thus starting the Brittany Spaniel. 71▶

Below: the Brittany Spaniel, a fine pointer and companion.

WELSH SPRINGER SPANIEL

Good points
- *Loyal*
- *Willing*
- *Fine gundog*
- *Excellent nose*
- *Good water dog*
- *Makes a good pet*

Take heed
- *Needs training or could become a destructive hunter*

The Welsh Springer Spaniel is a lively dog with plenty of enthusiasm and endurance. It is somewhere between the little Cocker Spaniel and the English Springer in stature. It is a tireless breed, and, in common with most spaniels, provided it is given plenty of exercise and correct feeding it will live to a ripe old age.

The Breed Standard states: 'A symmetrical, compact, strong, merry very active dog; not stilty (i.e. stiff in appearance); obviously built for endurance and hard work. A quick and active mover displaying plenty of push and drive.'

Size
Dog up to 48cm (19in) in height at shoulder, and bitch 46cm (18in) approximately.

Exercise
Like most spaniels the Welsh Springer is essentially a working animal and is not ideally suited for apartment life or for those with insufficient time to take it for lengthy walks.

Grooming
Similar care to other spaniels, with regular brushing and combing to maintain smartness.

Feeding
Recommended would be 1-1½ cans (376g, 13.3oz size) of a branded meaty product, with biscuit added in equal part by volume; or 3 cupfuls of a dry, complete diet mixed in the proportion of 1 cup of feed to ½ cup of hot or cold water.

Origin and history
A dog that would seem to be a forerunner of the Welsh Springer Spaniel is mentioned in the earliest records of the Laws of Wales, circa AD 1300, and indeed it appears that even before that time a similar white spaniel with red markings had been associated with the region. The Welsh Springer Spaniel is, in fact, very similar to the Brittany Spaniel, and makes a first-class gundog and household pet. 71▶

Below: The hard-working and very willing Welsh Springer Spaniel.

WETTERHOUN (Dutch Water Spaniel)

Good points
- *Excellent watchdog*
- *Fearless*
- *Hardworking*
- *Impervious to weather conditions*
- *Intelligent*

Take heed
- *Somewhat aggressive— needs firm handling*

The Wetterhoun, or Dutch Water Spaniel, was registered in Holland in 1942. However, it was known for many years before that, although then, as now, almost exclusively in Holland. It is an intelligent and fearless hunter, and is now often kept as a household companion. However, its somewhat aggressive nature, inherited from years of hunting, makes firm early training necessary.

Size
Height at withers: dog about 54.5cm (21½in); bitch should be slightly smaller.

Exercise
Needs plenty of exercise.

Grooming
Regular brushing will be sufficient.

Feeding
One to 1½ cans (376g, 13.3oz size) of a branded meaty product, with biscuit added in equal part by volume; or 3 cupfuls of a dry food, complete diet, mixed in the proportion of 1 cup of feed to ½ cup of hot or cold water.

Origin and history
Bred from dogs used for otter hunting, the Wetterhoun has evolved as a strong and fearless hunter, much prized as a guard dog. It has in the past been crossed with the Stabyhoun, but is a larger, sturdier dog.

Below: The Wetterhoun is a popular guard and farm dog in its native Holland; its dense curly coat is impervious to bad weather. It is also kept as a household companion.

BASSET HOUND

Good points
- *Distinctive appearance*
- *Equable temperament*
- *Good with children*
- *Ideal family pet*
- *Successful show dog*

Take heed
- *Needs lots of exercise*
- *Likes to wander*
- *Has a will of its own!*

The Basset Hound is an affable dog that gets on with most people and makes the ideal family pet. It does, however, retain strong hound instincts and will wander miles if a gate is left conveniently open. Basset owners are always telling folk about their Basset's roamings, often quite far afield, but it is up to them to see that their properties are adequately fenced. Like the Beagle, the Basset has a mind of its own; it is eminently lovable, but not always obedient.

Size
Height: 33-38cm (13-15in).

Exercise
Most important. If you can't give a Basset Hound plenty of exercise, don't have one.

Grooming
Daily brushing and combing. Pay attention to ears and toe-nails.

Feeding
One to 1½ cans (376g, 13.3oz size) of a branded meaty product, with biscuit added in equal part by volume; or 3 cupfuls of a dry food, complete diet, mixed in the proportion of 1 cup of feed to ½ cup of hot or cold water. Careful feeding in puppyhood is advocated for this fast-growing breed.

Health care
Choose the specimen with the straightest limbs, even if those knobbly knees seem attractive.

Origin and history
The Basset Hound is of French

Above: The friendly Basset Hound is renowned for its appealing but definitely soulful expression.

origin, being derived from the French Basset Artésien Normand, which was imported to England and crossed with the Bloodhound. It is a slow but sure tracker, still used in Britain to hunt hare. Primarily, however, it is kept as a popular household pet. French sources maintain that the first Bassets appeared in a litter of normal long-legged hounds, and that in breeding from these the Basset (which means 'dwarf') Hound appeared. 73▶

BASSET GRIFFON VENDÉEN

Good points
- *Excellent family pet*
- *Friendly*
- *Likes human company*
- *Voice will deter unwelcome callers*

Take heed
- *Needs plenty of exercise*
- *Not suitable for apartments or tiny gardens*

The Basset Griffon Vendéen (Petit) is an ancient French hunting breed. As its name implies, it is a short-legged (basset) rough-coated (griffon) hound, originating in the district of Vendée, and is one of the four breeds of Basset Hounds found in France, the others being the Basset Artésien Normand, the Basset Bleu de Gascogne, and the Basset Fauve de Bretagne.

The Basset Griffon Vendéen (Petit) is a cheerful, active, busy little hound, intelligent and inquisitive. Its friendly nature and liking for human companionship make it an excellent family pet, and its deep resonant voice is a deterrent to unwelcome callers.

Size
Height: 34-38cm (13½-15in). A tolerance of 1cm (²/₅in) is allowed.

Exercise
The Basset Griffon Vendéen (Petit) is an active, energetic breed needing plenty of exercise, and is not recommended for life in small apartments or houses with tiny gardens unless great care, time and trouble can be given to its needs and well-being.

Grooming
Its rough coat needs little attention.

Feeding
Recommended would be ½-1 can (376g, 13.3oz size) of a branded, meaty product, with biscuit added in equal part by volume; or 1½ cupfuls of a dry food, complete diet, mixed in the proportion of 1 cup of feed to ½ cup of hot or cold water.

Origin and history
The Griffon Vendéen (Petit) [to quote Monsieur P. Doubigne, an expert on the breed] is a miniature Basset reduced in size and proportions, while retaining all the qualities of the breed: the passion for hunting, fearlessness in the densest coverts, activity and vigour. It was bred down from a larger variety, the Basset Griffon Vendéen (Grand), which was originally used for wolf hunting and is now used, in France, for hunting wild boar. 72▶

BASSET ARTÉSIEN NORMAND

The Basset Artésien Normand is virtually identical to the Basset Hound and has the same feeding and grooming requirements and general characteristics. It is of ancient French origin, descended from the old French Bloodhound and the St Hubert Hound.

This breed found favour as a hunting dog in France, but was adopted by the British, who crossed it with the Bloodhound to develop the Basset Hound.

The breed stands 25-33cm (10-13in) high. Colours are white or white and orange. A tricoloured dog must be widely marked, with tan on the head and a mantle of specks of black or badger colour. 72▶

SWISS HUNTING DOGS (Schweizer Laufhund, Bruno de Jura, Lucernese, Bernese)

Good points
- Active
- Friendly
- First-rate hunting dogs

Take heed
- Not really suitable as household companions because of their lively disposition and hunting instincts

Schweizer Laufhund

There are some four varieties of the Swiss Hunting Dog (not to be confused with smaller types), all of which, with the exception of the Jura, have the same standard in their country of origin. They are friendly, active and powerfully built. They predominantly hunt hare and are speedy and excellent trackers with a good nose. Their lively disposition and strong hunting instincts do not equip them for the role of household companion.

Size
Minimum height: 44.5cm (17½in) all types, but varies considerably.

Exercise
Need plenty of vigorous exercise for full fitness.

Grooming
Regular brushing.

Feeding
One to 1½ cans (376g, 13.3oz size) of a branded meaty product, with biscuit added in equal part by volume; or 3 cupfuls of a dry food, complete diet, mixed in the proportion of 1 cup of feed to ½ cup of hot or cold water. This should be increased when the hound is in hard exercise.

Origin and history
The Swiss Hound, particularly the Laufhund, is a breed previously little known, but now gaining recognition internationally. To trace the origin of the Swiss Hounds we must go back to the pre-Christian era, when similar hunting dogs were introduced into

Above: A powerfully built Bernese Laufhund, one of the four types of Swiss Hunting Dogs. All are excellent hunters, with a keen sense of smell and a lively enthusiasm for the hunt.

Egypt by the Phoenicians and the Greeks, eventually finding their way to Switzerland when it was under Roman rule. The antiquity of the breed is verified by illustrations made during the 12th century, which can be seen in Zurich Cathedral. The heaviest of the four is the Jura, which is of the St Hubert type and similar to the French Ardennes Hound. When it gets the scent, it will brief with a drawn-out note that can be heard for many miles around: in fact it is rather like the English Bloodhound. The Bruno type of Jura is about the same size but appears sleeker and faster. 72▶

NORWEGIAN BUHUND (Norsk Buhund)

Good points
- *Alert and active*
- *Intelligent*
- *Full of stamina*
- *Friendly*
- *Gentle with children*
- *Good guard*

Take heed
- *Natural herder*
- *Needs plenty of exercise*

The Norwegian Buhund is a lively and alert dog, but a natural herder that will, like the Border Collie, round up anything, be it poultry, cattle or people. It needs lots of exercise and makes the ideal playmate for children.

Size
Dog not more than 45cm (17¾in); bitch somewhat less.

Exercise
Needs plenty of exercise to unleash its boundless energy.

Grooming
Regular brushing and combing. Easy breed to prepare for showing.

Feeding
One to 1½ cans (376g, 13.3oz size) of a branded meaty product, with biscuit added in equal part by volume; or 3 cupfuls of a dry food, complete diet, mixed in the proportion of 1 cup of feed to ½ cup of hot or cold water.

Origin and history
The Buhund is one of Norway's national dogs and was developed as an all-purpose farm dog to control sheep and cattle. It is, however, only since the 1920s that the breed has become known and appreciated outside its homeland, particularly in the United Kingdom, where it is gaining in popularity. It is likely that the Norrbotten Spitz, named after the northern region of Sweden, derives from Norwegian Buhund ancestry. 73▶

Below: The Norwegian Buhund requires lots of daily exercise.

KEESHOND

Good points
- Equable temperament
- Good watchdog
- Long-lived
- Adapts well as house pet
- Very loyal to owner

Take heed
- Needs lots of grooming
- One-person dog
- Loud bark

The Keeshond, Holland's national dog, began life as a barge dog, and still has the knack of finding an out-of-the-way corner for itself. It is a loyal dog, of sound temperament, but needs a lot of grooming and tends to favour one member of the family. It is an excellent watchdog and generally has a very long life.

Size
Height: dog 46cm (18in), bitch 43cm (17in).

Exercise
Average requirements.

Grooming
Regular attention with a stiff brush. A choke chain should not be used on this breed or it will spoil the ruff.

Feeding
Recommended would be 1-1½ cans (376g, 13.3oz size) of a branded meaty product, with biscuit added in equal part by volume; or 3 cupfuls of a dry food, complete diet, mixed in the proportion of 1 cup of feed to ½ cup of hot or cold water.

Origin and history
The Keeshond (plural Keeshonden), pronounced Kayshond, has a romantic history. During the period of uncertainty that preceded the French Revolution, the patriots were led by a man named Kees de Gyselaer, a dog lover who owned a little dog of this breed. The dog, named Kees, became the symbol of the patriots, and gave the breed its name.

Above: The loyal Keeshond adapts well as a house pet, being happy to curl up in a corner. Its acute hearing and loud bark make it an excellent watchdog.

The Keeshond has never become very popular outside Holland, despite Mrs I. Tucker's Champion Volkrijk of Vorden being Best in Show at Crufts in 1957. It has, however, a staunch band of devotees who breed for soundness and quality. In common with other Spitz varieties, the Keeshond must originally have evolved in the Arctic Circle, and it has the traditional Spitz tail tightly curled over the back. 73▶

LAPPHUND (Lapland Spitz)

Good points
- *Easy to train*
- *Friendly*
- *Lively*
- *Courageous*
- *Intelligent*
- *Good guard dog*

Take heed
- *Suspicious of strangers*

The Lapphund was bred to hunt reindeer, but since the need for this type of work has ceased, the breed has been used not only as a cattle dog, but also as a household pet, a role into which it has fitted happily, being both friendly and easy to train.

Size
Height: dog 44.5-49.5cm (17½-19½in) at the shoulder; bitch 39.5-44.5cm (15½-17½in).

Exercise
Needs regular walks and off-the-lead runs for full fitness.

Grooming
Regular brushing will keep the coat in good condition.

Feeding
One to 1½ cans (376g, 13.3oz

Above: The Lapphund, popular in its native Sweden, was once a herder of reindeer but has now become a pet and guard dog.

size) of a branded meaty product, with biscuit added in equal part by volume; or 3 cupfuls of a dry food, complete diet, mixed in the proportion of 1 cup of feed to ½ cup of hot or cold water.

Origin and history
The Lapphund was produced as a hunter and herder of reindeer. When the reindeer became a farm animal, the Lapphund was given a new role as a cattle dog, but a larger number found their way to the south of Sweden, where they began to be kept as family pets. The breed is slowly but surely becoming very popular in its country of origin. 73▶

WACHTELHUND (German Spaniel; German Quail Dog)

Good points
- Excellent nose
- Good in water
- Fine retriever/gundog
- Hardy
- Fine sporting companion
- Good guard dog

Take heed
- No drawbacks known

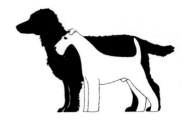

The Wachtelhund is a hardy breed bearing some resemblance to the English Springer Spaniel. It is little known outside Germany, where it has a sound reputation as a gundog and retriever.

Size
Height: 39.5-49.5cm (15½-19½in).

Exercise
Needs plenty of exercise.

Grooming
Normal daily brushing.

Feeding
One to 1½ cans (376g, 13.3oz size) of a branded meaty product, with biscuit added in equal part by volume; or 3 cupfuls of a dry food, complete diet, mixed in the pro-portion of 1 cup of feed to ½ cup of hot or cold water.

Origin and history
The Germans, when they produced the Wachtelhund, wanted to create a breed that could cope with waters and forest and also flush out and retrieve game. The breed was produced by the crossing of a number of small dogs. However, Harrap's *Champion Dogs of the World* credits the old German Stöber with the Wachtelhund's excellent nose, the Stöber having had tracking ability similar to the Bloodhound.

The Wachtelhund, which is not recognized in either the United Kingdom or the USA, is usually dark brown in colour and there can be white marks on chest and toes. It can also be white with brown spots, white and brown, or solid white in colour

Below: The Wachtelhund, or German Spaniel, is at home in the fields flushing out and retrieving game.

PORTUGUESE WARREN HOUND

Good points
- *Attractive*
- *Choice of size*
- *First-class hunter*
- *Affectionate*
- *Intelligent*
- *Alert*
- *Good watchdog*

Take heed
- *No drawbacks known*

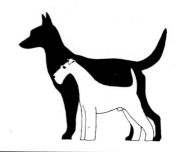

In its native land, the Portuguese Warren Hound is known as the Podengo. It is fairly rare, although by no means unknown, outside Portugal, where it is popular both as a companion and as a hunter of rabbits, hares and even deer. It comes in three sizes, the Podengo Pequeno, which resembles a rather large, smooth-coated Chihuahua, a larger (Medio) variety, and the biggest, which more closely resembles the Spanish Ibizan Hound, the Podenco Ibicenco.

Size
The Podengo Pequeno (small) stand 20-30cm (8-12in) high at the shoulder, the Podengo Medio (medium) stand 51-56cm (20-22in), and the Podengo Grande (large) stands 56-68.5cm (22-27in) high.

Exercise
Happiest when given plenty of exercise.

Grooming
Regular brushing is needed. A velvet pad will also improve the appearance of the coat.

Feeding
For the small Podengo ½-1 can (376g, 13.3oz size) of a branded meaty product with biscuit added in equal part by volume; or 1½ cupfuls of a dry food, complete diet, mixed in the proportion of 1 cup of feed to ½ cup of hot or cold water. For the medium-sized Podengo, 1-1½ cans of a branded meaty product of similar dimensions, with biscuit added in equal part by volume; or 3 cupfuls of a dry food, complete diet, mixed in the proportion of 1 cup of feed to ½ cup of hot or cold water. The large variety should receive 1½-2½ cans of a branded meaty product, of similar dimensions, with biscuit added in equal part by volume; or 5 cupfuls of a dry food, complete diet, mixed in the proportion of 1 cup of feed to ½ cup of hot or cold water.

Origin and history
The Podengo is well established in its own country, where the small variety, the Pequeno, is used for rabbiting and also for hunting hares; the medium variety also hunts rabbits and hares while the larger dog is used for hunting deer. There is an infusion of blood from a number of gazehounds and although the Pequeno is closely allied to the Chihuahua, the larger variety resembles the Ibizan Hound.

This dog is not currently recognized by the AKC, the UK KC or the FCI. However, it is usually fawn in colour and can be rough- or smooth-coated. Other coat colours are yellow, brown, grey-black or sooty, with or without white spots.

The breed is shown at Portuguese dog shows, but is rarely seen in other countries. Very popular with the country people of Portugal, the Warren Hound may be owned as a single dog or kept in a pack for hunting purposes. The larger varieties are usually hunted singly or in pairs, while the small variety is taken out in a pack. 74▶

PORTUGUESE WATER DOG (Cão d'Agua)

Good points
- *Strongly built*
- *Active*
- *Excellent retriever*
- *First-rate swimmer*
- *Good watchdog*
- *Loyal*

Take heed
- *Suspicious of strangers*

The Portuguese Water Dog is most commonly found in the Algarve area of its native Portugal where it is a true fisherman's dog, acting virtually as a member of the crew and tackling a variety of tasks ranging from guarding the nets to diving and retrieving; it will actually catch an escaping fish in its jaws and swim back with it safely to the boat. It is loyal to its master, but not very trustworthy with strangers.

Size
Height: dog 51-57cm (20-22½in); bitch 43-52cm (17-20½in). Weight: dog 19-25kg (42-55lb); bitch 15.9-22kg (35-48½lb).

Exercise
Revels in an active, outdoor life.

Grooming
The Portuguese Water Dog comes in two coat types, but as this is the only difference there is only one standard for the breed. There is a long-coated variety, which has a lion show trim reminiscent of the Poodle; and a short curly-coated variety, which gives the animal an appealingly scruffy appearance, particularly as it is so often in water. Regular brushing is advised to maintain smartness.

Feeding
One to 1½ cans (376g, 13.3oz size) of a branded meaty product, with biscuit added in equal part by volume; or 3 cupfuls of a dry food, complete diet, mixed in the proportion of 1 cup of feed to ½ cup of hot or cold water.

Above: The Portuguese Water Dog is now mainly found in the Algarve.

Origin and history
This unusual dog, which is not only a fine fisherman but can also catch rabbits, has been known for centuries around the Iberian Peninsula, where it was bred for its task of retrieving fish and guarding nets. Formerly used throughout Portugal, it is almost limited today to the region of the Algarve, where fishing traditions continue very much as in the past. It is little known outside its country of origin. This breed should not be confused with the Portuguese Warren Hound (or Podengo), which is mainly found in Northern Portugal, where it is used for hunting rabbits and other animals. 74

POINTING WIRE - HAIRED GRIFFON

Good points
- *Strongly built*
- *Easy to train*
- *Equable temperament*
- *Good companion*
- *Intelligent*

Take heed
- *A reliable and careful, rather than speedy, gundog*

The Pointing Wire-haired Griffon is an intelligent, companionable dog that not only points, but also works well in water. It is an attractive, good-natured animal, which performs its task slowly but surely. It is easily trained.

Size
Height: dog 54.5-60cm (21½-23½in), bitch 49.5-54.5cm (19½-21½in).

Exercise
Needs plenty of vigorous exercise.

Grooming
Regular brushing will keep the coat in good condition.

Feeding
One to 1½ cans (376g, 13.3oz size) of a branded meaty product, with biscuit added in equal part by volume; or 3 cupfuls of a dry food, complete diet, mixed in the proportion of 1 cup of feed to ½ cup of hot or cold water.

Origin and history
The Pointing Wire-haired Griffon was developed around 1874 by a Dutch sportsman named Edward Korthals. Korthals was a man of considerable breeding experience, who had managed the kennels of a German prince for many years, and it was his resolve to produce a dog with both courage and hunting ability. He achieved this by experimental crossings with French, Belgian and German gundogs until the Pointing Wire-haired Griffon was established — a pointer that was at home in water and, although not as swift a worker as other gundogs, a reliable and plucky worker. Some say that it is the ideal gundog for the older sportsman. It was first shown in the United Kingdom in 1888. 74▶

Below: The slow but reliable Pointing Wire-haired Griffon. It is known in the USA as the Wire-haired Pointing Griffon.

Index

Page numbers in Roman type refer to text entries; *italic* numbers refer to photographs; **bold** numbers to colour artwork illustrations.